D0388475

"If you or someone you love is struggling with the fear and uncertainty of living in cancer's shadow, here's your flashlight."

DAVE DRAVECKY (desmoid cancer survivor since 1988)
Dave Dravecky's Outreach of Hope Ministry
Colorado Springs, Colorado

"Our life was forever changed when we each received a cancer diagnosis, but this change has not necessarily been for the worse. Both of us have experienced the necessity of reordering our lives around new priorities. The stories in *Finding the Light in Cancer's Shadow* are *our* stories. Relying on a faith community for support, finding joy in each day, believing that we are 'survivors,' and trusting God in all things are hallmarks of the experience of living in cancer's shadow. We commend Lynn Eib for her powerful collection of witnesses to hope."

GEORGE GALLUP (prostate cancer survivor since 1993)
KINGSLEY GALLUP (breast cancer survivor since 1999)
The George H. Gallup International Institute
Princeton, New Jersey

"Anxieties about cancer don't end after treatment. No one knows that better than cancer survivor and patient advocate Lynn Eib. She has written a much-needed resource for those living in the shadow of this life-threatening disease."

HAROLD G. KOENIG, MD
Professor of psychiatry and behavioral sciences
Founder and co-director, Center for Spirituality, Theology and Health
Duke University
Durham, North Carolina

"As a family physician who has cared for and walked alongside cancer patients for almost thirty years, I am always on the lookout for resources that bring hope and increase faith in the midst of the despair of this devastating diagnosis. This book is not only one that brought me peace and comfort to read but will be one I can enthusiastically recommend to my patients—and to you."

WALT LARIMORE, MD
Family physician, medical journalist, and best-selling author of God's Design for the Highly Healthy Person

"This extraordinary book is inspirational, uplifting, and comforting to anyone facing a cancer diagnosis and to those ministering to them. Lynn remains steadfast and faithful as she shares her gift of bonding with humanity, while always trusting God's will."

JANE E. RICE (breast cancer survivor since 1990)
Vice president, public relations
Utz Quality Foods, Inc.
Hanover, Pennsylvania

"Lynn Eib brings her unique blend of credibility, personal vulnerability, and clinical perspective to help patients and caregivers struggling to find meaning and hope in the midst of cancer. Her book addresses the practical questions that cancer brings and discusses the issues plainly and without jargon. Yet *Finding the Light in Cancer's Shadow* is much more than a practical manual of how to deal with this disease. Lynn points the way out of the trap of 'cured vs. not-cured' to a freedom and peace based on faith in the One who is finally bigger than cancer."

PETER G. RUEHLMAN, MD
Medical oncologist
Cincinnati, Ohio

FINDING THE LIGHT IN CANCER'S SHADOW

Lynn Eib

Tyndale House Publishers, Inc.
Carol Stream, Illinois

Visit Tyndale's exciting Web site at www.tyndale.com

TYNDALE is a registered trademark of Tyndale House Publishers, Inc.

Tyndale's quill logo is a trademark of Tyndale House Publishers, Inc.

Finding the Light in Cancer's Shadow

Copyright © 2006 by Lynn Eib. All rights reserved.

Cover photograph of man walking copyright © by The Image Bank/Getty Images. All rights reserved.

Author photo copyright © 2004 by Steve Lock. All rights reserved.

Designed by Cathy Bergstrom

Edited by Kimberly Miller

Unless otherwise indicated, all Scripture quotations are taken from the *Holy Bible*, New Living Translation, second edition, copyright © 1996, 2004. Used by permission of Tyndale House Publishers, Inc., Carol Stream, Illinois 60188. All rights reserved.

Scripture quotations marked NLT-1 are taken from the *Holy Bible*, New Living Translation, first edition, copyright © 1996. Used by permission of Tyndale House Publishers, Inc., Carol Stream, Illinois 60188. All rights reserved.

Scripture quotations marked NIV are taken from the *Holy Bible*, New International Version®. NIV®. Copyright © 1973, 1978, 1984 by International Bible Society. Used by permission of Zondervan. All rights reserved.

Scripture quotations marked NASB are taken from the *New American Standard Bible*, © 1960, 1962, 1963, 1968, 1971, 1972, 1973, 1975, 1977, 1995 by The Lockman Foundation. Used by permission.

Note from the author: To protect the privacy of certain patients and their family members, some names and other details have been altered.

Library of Congress Cataloging-in-Publication Data

Eib, Lynn.
     Finding the light in cancer's shadow / Lynn Eib.
       p. cm.
     Includes bibliographical references.
     ISBN-13: 978-1-4143-0572-1 (sc)
     ISBN-10: 1-4143-0572-9 (sc)
     1. Cancer—Patients—Religious life.   2. Cancer—Religious aspects—Christianity.   3. Eib, Lynn.
I. Title.

     BV4910.33.E36 2006
     248.8'6196994—dc22   2005026400

Printed in the United States of America

10   09   08   07   06
8   7   6   5   4   3   2   1

DEDICATION

*This book is lovingly dedicated
to my parents,
Robert and Gaynor Yoxtheimer,
with much thanks
for first showing me the light;
and to my brother,
Jim,
with much joy
for our walk together in the light.*

TABLE OF CONTENTS

ACKNOWLEDGMENTS

I used to say "I could never write a book," and here you are holding a copy of my *second* book. I will never cease to be amazed at God's ability to do "immeasurably more than all we ask or imagine" (Ephesians 3:20, NIV).

I would like to say **THANK YOU**:

To the love of my life, my husband, Ralph, whose encouragement and prayers keep enabling me to be all that God meant me to be.

To my beautiful daughters, Lindsey, Bethany, and Danielle, who continue to enthusiastically support my writing endeavors and are grateful I have found a means to pay for their weddings!

To my son-in-law, Josh, for being the answer to a mother's prayer for her daughter.

To my oncologist/boss/brother in Messiah, Marc Hirsh, who had the wisdom to see what God wanted to do with my life and provided me with the opportunity to do it.

To my prayer partner/dear friend Elizabeth Hirsh, who has lifted my needs regularly to the Lord, prayed for all of you who would one day read this book, and proofread my manuscript.

To all the cancer survivors and their families, who allowed me to share their true stories of hope, humor, and healing.

To all the members of my cancer and grief prayer support groups, who constantly prove to me that God can and will meet our deepest needs.

To my Wise Women of Esther prayer partners, Carolyn Dunn and Janice Smith, and all the ladies in my WWE groups, who prayed for so many aspects of this book and often hold up my weary arms when I am in the "battle."

To my church family at Christ's American Baptist, whose prayers have uplifted and empowered my ministry to cancer patients and their families.

To my friend and fellow cancer survivor Louis Koschmeder, who read my manuscript and made very helpful comments and suggestions.

To ophthalmologist Dr. John Hutton, who took time to verify some of my medical details about tears.

And to the Knox Group at Tyndale House, who believed in my message (again!) and treats me so wonderfully; especially associate publisher for books Janis Long Harris, manuscript editor Kim Miller, and author relations manager Sharon Leavitt.

Have you ever been driving down the road when all of a sudden you hit a patch of "black ice"? If you live in a climate that experiences true winter, you know exactly what I mean.

You're cruising merrily along on bare pavement one minute and sliding down the road the next instant. You're on black ice—a covering of ice so thin that the dark pavement still shows through. If you apply the brakes, they do nothing to stop your vehicle. Instead you just keep sliding, maybe even sideways, until you find something *bigger* than you to stop your slide!

When I was diagnosed with metastatic colon cancer in 1990 at the age of thirty-six, I felt as if I had hit a huge patch of black ice. I had been going merrily along in life—happily married to my pastor-husband and enjoying our three daughters, then eight, ten, and twelve. I loved my career as a newspaper reporter and even found time to exercise regularly at the local Y.

I consider myself an organized, well-prepared person, but . . . I never saw the black ice of cancer ahead of me.

It took me so by surprise that I couldn't even think how to react.

I tapped the brakes and nothing happened. I still had cancer.
I pressed a little harder on the brakes, and I found out the
    cancer had spread to my lymph nodes.

I slammed on the brakes only to learn that the odds I would
survive were less than the odds I wouldn't.

I was sliding sideways, out of control, and it was the scariest time
of my life. Thankfully, I didn't crash, but I did find something bigger
than me to stop my slide.

Actually Someone.

I slid right into the big, open arms of a loving God, and He
assured me that He had seen the black ice coming and was waiting
all along to stop my slide. I prayed He would just make the black ice
disappear so I could be carefree once again, but He didn't. So I continued riding on the thin layer of black ice through surgery and six
months of weekly chemotherapy, which included having to endure
a drug to which I was allergic.

Eventually the ice melted and I started driving along again,
although it wasn't quite as merrily, because once you've hit a really
big, really bad patch of black ice, you never forget it. You're a little
afraid you're going to hit another patch and pretty paranoid that
every black shadow on the road just *might* be some more ice—even
if it's summer!

Once I finished my treatments, I was relieved not to be on black
ice anymore, but now it seemed as if the disease was a shadow hanging over my life as I wondered and worried when and if it might
return. I felt a little like the Peanuts cartoon character Pigpen—you
know, the poor guy who always had a big cloud of black dust following him wherever he went!

That's what this book is about: living in the shadow of cancer.
I've written it for the nearly *10 million of us* (and our families) who
have heard the words "you have cancer," have finished our recommended treatment, and now must try to return to life-after-a-cancer-

diagnosis. Some of us have been told the cancer is gone; others may be in a remission wondering how long it will last. Still others may know the illness is a chronic condition that will require treatment again.

Whatever kind of shadow we're under, I believe it is possible to find the light. And I don't think we have to wait until we've reached the "magic five-year mark" or until we are pronounced officially cured or until we get a durable remission. I believe we can find the light every single day, hour, and minute we live as cancer survivors.

To me, being a cancer survivor can mean living cancer-free, living in remission, or living with the disease. The common factor is that we are *living* and therefore are survivors!

One of the strange things about a cancer diagnosis is that often it can be *more* difficult to live as a cancer survivor *after* treatment than during it—not the physical part of dealing with cancer, but the emotional and spiritual sides of it.

I was definitely not prepared for this in my cancer journey. I thought when I finished surgery and chemo, I would be deliriously happy and cancer would be a distant memory. I was pretty joyful— until I saw the shadow lurking over me. My oncologist told me that even though my cancer had been successfully removed through surgery, there was a high probability it would recur because it had spread to several lymph nodes. At the time I completed chemo in early 1991, there was no approved drug regimen for colon cancer other than the one I already had used. There were absolutely no approved drugs for recurrent colon cancer, and procedures such as liver and lung resections for spread colon cancer were extremely rare. I had had my one and only shot at being cured.

"If the cancer does comes back, it probably will come back within two years and you will die very quickly," my doctor told me.

Now that's one nasty shadow.

I tried various methods to get rid of cancer's shadow. I closed my eyes very tightly: *I don't see any shadow.* But it was very hard to go through a normal day with my eyes closed.

I got very busy. *The shadow won't be able to catch up with me.* But shadows are much faster than I realized.

I thought positive. *That's not a shadow. It's a big, happy, black balloon!* But it sure was dark under there.

I had so many questions swirling around my mind, and each one made the shadow seem more menacing: *When do I know I'm a survivor? How do I turn off that little voice of fear? Do I positively have to stay positive?* And the really big one: *Will the cancer come back?*

What I've learned over the years is that there are answers to those hard questions, and when we know those answers, we can find the light in cancer's shadow. I've experienced it in my own life and have seen hundreds of other cancer survivors and their loved ones discover it too.

That's because in 1996 my cancer journey took another turn. My oncologist, Dr. Marc Hirsh, offered me a job as a patient advocate, providing emotional and spiritual support to his cancer patients and their caregivers. I now look at my job as getting in the car with *other* people who are driving and sliding on black ice.

You're probably thinking: *Who would want a job like that?* That's what I would have said too, six years earlier when I was first diagnosed with cancer. But in those intervening years, God slowly had given me a desire to reach out to those with cancer. Actually, I had been praying I could quit my public-relations job and *volunteer* to work with cancer patients, but I knew that wasn't financially feasible with college looming for our daughters.

As you can imagine, I was pretty excited when Marc offered to *pay* me for something I had been praying about doing for free! He and his wife, Elizabeth, had become close friends of ours in the years since my diagnosis, and he often sent his patients to the prayer support group for cancer patients that I had founded in the fall of 1991. Marc said he offered me the job as patient advocate because he could see the calling of God on my life.

Now that's a scary phrase: "the calling of God."

I just wanted to encourage cancer patients and help them believe God could meet their deepest needs. I hadn't thought about actually getting into the car with them while they were sliding on black ice!

But that's what I do every workday in Marc's office. It's a really unusual arrangement—perhaps even unique in this country—to have someone like me right in the office to listen, talk, pray, and encourage those facing cancer. Marc, a Messianic Jew, and I have spoken about faith and medicine at medical conferences all around the country and have yet to meet another physician who employs someone with a job like mine.

As I write this, I have met nearly 1,500 newly diagnosed cancer patients in our office. I've had hundreds more attend my biweekly support group (which I've discovered is one of the oldest—if not *the* oldest—continuously meeting faith-based cancer support group in the country). Through e-mails, calls, and letters, I've also "met" scores of cancer patients who read my first book, *When God & Cancer Meet.* If there were an entry in the Guinness Book of World Records for having the most friends and acquaintances with cancer, I would definitely be in the running!

Chances are that you and I probably will never meet, but I'd like to offer to get in the car with you as you anxiously survey the shadows on the road for black ice or furtively glance in your rearview mirror to see what's following you. Don't worry, I'm not going to try to drive. I'll just buckle up as we ride together, and I'll help you hear from the One who does know how to navigate on this often treacherous journey.

Just the other day my youngest daughter, Lindsey, told me that she was driving in a snowstorm with a friend. She started sliding on some ice and was really frightened. Her natural reaction was to slam on the brakes or jerk the steering wheel the other way. But her friend kept calmly reminding her of truths like "turn into the skid" and "just tap the brakes." They arrived at their destination safely, and she was so thankful he was in the car with her.

I don't know exactly where you or your loved one is along your cancer journey. Maybe you've been blindsided fairly recently by the black ice of cancer. Maybe you're still slamming on the brakes trying to believe it isn't so. Perhaps you're scared because you can't steer the way you want to go. Maybe you're waiting for the crash and are half-afraid to open your eyes. Perhaps you see shadows of black ice down every road.

I don't care how big the cancer was, how small your cure odds are, how little time a doctor says you or your loved one has, I have a message for you: God is bigger than cancer and His light is brighter than cancer's shadow.

This book is full of true stories about cancer survivors I know and how I have seen them not only survive, but thrive in the weeks, months, and years since their cancer diagnoses. Nearly all are cancer-free, but all of them are *free-of-cancer*. That's an important distinction.

While there are many things we can do to improve our chances of being cured of cancer, I do not believe there is any way to *guarantee* that outcome. I do, however, believe that all of us living in the shadow of cancer—whether the disease has struck us or a loved one—can be free of the icy grip it can have over our minds and spirits. Our lives can be filled with peace and hope: free-of-cancer.

I don't think we can ever hear that message too many times. The people I know facing cancer never tire of hearing true, hope-filled stories about others facing this life-threatening disease. I've used their stories to try to answer the questions we cancer survivors most often ask. Hearing their stories reminds us that others have walked a similar path, felt similar emotions, and endured similar sufferings. And most of all, their stories remind us that we don't have to fear the black ice of cancer in our rearview mirror because God wants desperately to show us His power, peace, and presence in the midst of our journeys.

If you already have enough hope and healing in your life, don't bother to read this book. But if you've got questions and would like to find the light in cancer's shadow, then unlock the car door, let me hop in, and keep reading!

CHAPTER 1

So, How Do I Know When I'm a Survivor?

This is a not a book for B.C. (Before Cancer).

And it's not really a book for A.D. (After Diagnosis).

It's a book for A.C.T. (After Cancer Treatment).

It's hope for life after cancer treatment. You or your loved one has survived surgery or chemotherapy or radiation or maybe all three. What do you do now?

You may have been told that the cancer is gone or in remission. You may know what the specific odds are that it will or won't recur. You may even be dealing with a kind of cancer that doctors say probably *will* come back.

So when do you know that you or your loved one is a survivor?

I was diagnosed June 26, 1990, with stage III colon cancer. I still am cancer-free and count myself as a very blessed survivor. Even if the cancer had returned, I would still count myself as a survivor because I agree with the National Coalition for Cancer Survivorship when it labels cancer patients as survivors "from the moment of diagnosis and for the balance of life."[1]

I didn't always think that way.

I used to think that you had to live five years after a diagnosis to be called a cancer survivor.

I remember going in for my five-year oncology checkup in the summer of 1995 (before I started working in Marc's office) and gleefully announcing to Marc that I wouldn't be seeing him professionally anymore. (I'm not quite sure how I got that notion, but I hear many others say the same kind of thing. We've probably made that association because statisticians often give data on five-year survival rates for different types of cancer.)

"Where did you get that idea?" Marc responded.

"It's five years; I'm cured!" I told him, surprised that he didn't realize it was such a momentous day.

"Well, the chance the cancer will return has diminished greatly, but you still need to be checked for the rest of your life," Marc soberly explained.

Talk about bursting someone's bubble!

I waited five years to be proclaimed a survivor and there was going to be no such official announcement.

Thankfully, a short time after that day, I read the above-mentioned survivorship definition from the National Coalition for Cancer Survivorship and proclaimed myself a survivor. (The National Cancer Institute Office of Cancer Survivorship also says that "an individual is considered a cancer survivor from the time of diagnosis through the balance of his or her life."[2])

So I hope you're not waiting for some mythical five-year mark to earn the label of cancer survivor. If you have survived even one minute since diagnosis, you already are a survivor!

But this hard earned label of cancer survivor brings with it a sobering reality: We have come face-to-face with a life-threatening disease. And as long as we wear that cancer survivor label, there will be checkups and blood tests and reminders that we are living in cancer's shadow. I believe that we can find the light even in cancer's dark shadow, but I don't believe it's a once-and-for-all experience that enables us to quickly move out from under this shadow. Rather it's something that we commit ourselves to continue doing for weeks, months, and usually years.

Did you ever sleep with a night-light when you were a little kid? (Maybe you still do as an adult—you don't have to tell me.) Our middle daughter, Bethany, had an insatiable need to sleep with a night-light until she was about eight or nine. She needed that light to reassure her that there were no scary shadows in her bedroom. Her dependence was so strong that when she was a toddler, if the night-light bulb burned out during the night, she would wake up crying. I never figured out how someone with her eyes closed could tell that the night-light wasn't on, but Bethany always could. We joked that she would need to take a night-light on her honeymoon, but eventually she learned to sleep in the dark.

I think cancer survivors are a lot like Bethany was as a little girl. We need constant reassurance that the dark shadows we see—or think we see—aren't going to get us. We want to know that our paranoia is normal, that our fears can be conquered, that it's okay to cry once in a while, and that there isn't any more black ice ahead.

We need to know the night-light is on.

The people you'll meet throughout this book are really quite average cancer survivors. They haven't won seven Tour de France races or accomplished another spectacular feat. They were all amazed when I said I wanted to interview them for this book, and most protested that they don't have it all together. And that's exactly why I picked them. They are real people with real feelings, and you'll be encouraged that if they can find the light, you can too. I met them all through my job as a patient advocate, and most also belong to my Cancer Prayer Support Group. Some have beaten the odds; others are planning for the future despite the odds. All have found a new appreciation for life.

❧ ❧ ❧

One of these survivors is my friend Claude. According to statistics, he didn't have much of a chance to survive his cancer diagnosis. The survival statistics on lung cancer are pretty dismal—especially when the tumor is inoperable, which his was.

The grim news came around Memorial Day 2000. Claude had finally kicked a fifty-year addiction to cigarettes and was looking forward to retiring in a few years from his job with a large utilities firm. Like most of us, he was shocked to get the pathology report.

"I felt dead inside," Claude recalls. "I remember the first doctor who said 'lung cancer' to me—it was like he was talking and I could hear his words, but it was as if he were talking to someone else."

Claude, then sixty, looked and felt quite fine. But there it was in black-and-white. The walnut-sized tumor was "poorly differentiated" and too near the heart and aorta for surgery. He agreed to try some chemo and radiation in hopes of shrinking the tumor and buying more time.

"Three different doctors told me to expect to live a year—two years if the treatment went really well," Claude says. "There was no prognosis of a future. They advised me to get my affairs in order."

Claude found himself with extra time after his employer decided he was permanently disabled several months after his diagnosis— despite the fact that Claude had continued to work throughout his "pretty rough" treatments.

The decision turned out to be a blessing in disguise, Claude says, because it allowed him to "retire" three years early. Instead of working at his job, Claude became a full-time volunteer, participating in community-service projects, organizing ministries at his church, and even traveling to Russia with his wife for a two-week mission trip to share his culture and his faith in the Russian schools.

"My wife and I have had the freedom to come and go and enjoy the things we always wanted to do," Claude explains.

Despite being told initially that he didn't have long to live, Claude says he thought of himself "as a survivor from the very beginning."

He says that his confidence as a survivor was bolstered after a large group of friends gathered around him and prayed for him at his church the week after his diagnosis. He didn't hear an audible voice or see any flash in the sky, but several phrases kept going through his head even as a peace settled in his heart.

"The words I heard in my mind were: 'Trust Me. I am able. Nothing is too difficult for Me,'" Claude says. "I knew in the very depth of my being that God had touched me and I didn't have anything to worry about.

"I just began to walk as a healed man, a healthy man," he adds.

Claude says he moved ahead with his planned medical treatments because he believed God was going to use them to bring about his cure, even though doctors had told him they didn't think a cure was medically possible.

Four years later, his lung cancer has not returned, and Claude insists that his life after lung cancer is "better than my life before."

He credits "good doctors and the good Lord" for healing the lung cancer.

"I have gotten physically stronger day after day and have been spiritually strengthened too," he says. "I appreciate everything around me more every day."

Still, Claude admits that he feels "a little apprehension" at each checkup.

"I never walk in [my oncologist's] office that my blood pressure doesn't go up a little," he says with a laugh. "It's like another moment of truth is here."

❧ ❧ ❧

My friend Blaine has had a few of his own moments of truth since his diagnosis of stage III esophageal cancer at the age of forty-two in March 2001.

Blaine is one of the healthiest-looking cancer patients I've ever met. He owns his own remodeling company and is an avid golfer. When diagnosed, he could scarcely believe he had cancer.

"I never knew anyone with cancer—I hardly knew what cancer was," he says.

Doctors decided to do neoadjuvant treatment—chemo and radiation before surgery—in hopes of greatly shrinking the tumor in his esophagus, which already had spread to the lymph nodes. Blaine had a continuous infusion pump implanted and got radiation every weekday while chemo pushed silently through his veins.

Many people with similar cancers are forced to get a feeding tube while receiving both chemo and radiation because swallowing can become very difficult. But a month after starting treatment, Blaine had lost only a few pounds and even sampled bowls of spicy beans at a chili cook-off at the nearby county fairgrounds.

In July the surgeon went in to remove the tumor—except there wasn't much of anything to remove. The treatment had worked so well that there was "only a small amount of residual disease," according to the surgeon's notes.

"When I woke up in intensive care, I knew I was a survivor," Blaine recalls.

The successful surgery increased his chances of a cure from about 30 percent to 70 percent, the surgeon told Blaine.

Given a second chance at life, Blaine and his wife, Becky, began to think more about their spiritual life together. "For fourteen years [of marriage] my wife and I discussed whether we should go to this church or that one, but we never did anything about it," Blaine explains. After the cancer diagnosis, they accepted a couple's invitation to a nearby church, became members, and even joined the choir just two months after Blaine's surgery.

Blaine still shakes his head in amazement as he considers how he, who never sang before his esophageal cancer, now looks forward to singing at his church. And despite the fact that every few months he has to have his throat dilated (a stretching procedure to keep it from becoming too tight), he even sings solos at his church. On the first Christmas Eve after his surgery, he sang "O Holy Night" and has sung a solo every year since on that sacred night. He even sings occasionally for our support group parties, and all who listen enjoy the heartfelt enthusiasm he conveys for each song's message.

Every time I read Psalm 40 I think of Blaine:

I waited patiently for the LORD to help me,
and he turned to me and heard my cry.
He lifted me out of the pit of despair,
out of the mud and the mire.
He set my feet on solid ground
and steadied me as I walked along.
He has given me a NEW SONG to sing,
a hymn of praise to our God.

Many will see what he has done and be amazed.

They will put their trust in the LORD.

PSALM 40:1-3 (emphasis mine)

Instead of dwelling under the shadow of cancer, Blaine has allowed God to put a new song in his heart.

෨෨   ෨෨   ෨෨

Bill and Jakoba (or "Jake" as her friends call her) know a thing or two about being under the shadow of cancer—this husband and wife were diagnosed with cancer just six weeks apart.

Jake got the dreaded news first in February 2002 when she was diagnosed at the age of sixty with breast cancer that had spread to the lymph nodes. After surgery to remove the lump, the couple decided to keep their plans for a short Florida vacation the next month.

"My whole goal was to be her nurse and help her recuperate," Bill recalls. "But on March 18 the world changed a bit."

That's the day an episode of bleeding sent Bill, then sixty-one, to a Florida emergency room where doctors discovered a cancerous tumor in his colon.

Doctors wanted him to remain in the Sunshine State and have immediate surgery, but Bill wanted to get back to Pennsylvania for his wife's first scheduled chemo treatment.

"My focus wasn't on my cancer; it was on Jake," he says.

So they took a flight headed back home, even though the emergency-room doctor had predicted Bill would die in flight. He immediately saw a local surgeon and was operated on for stage III colorectal cancer.

They aren't the first husband-wife duo to have chemo together in our office, but they probably are the one with the most positive attitudes.

When they finished their respective treatments, both felt very optimistic that "we really beat this thing," Bill says.

More than three years later, Jake continued to be cancer-free, but about a year after finishing treatment, Bill's routine blood work showed his CEA tumor marker (a blood test that may indicate a recurrence of colon cancer) was elevated, and subsequent scans indicated the cancer had spread to the liver.

The three of us talked in my office after they got the news. Both were quite shaken and had a big concern: In a few months Bill was running for an international position with the Lions Club, the world's largest service organization dedicated especially to helping the blind and visually impaired.

As we talked, Bill said he thought it probably would be best to turn down the nomination because the high-level position would require extensive traveling in and out of the country. They also were scheduled to leave in eleven days for a Lions Club meeting in Portland, Oregon, and decided to forgo that trip.

But in the ensuing days as they talked and prayed about their future, both felt a peace about Bill continuing to campaign and run for the office.

"I told her I was going to run—whatever happened [with the cancer] was going to happen, so why should I just sit back and wait for it?" Bill recalls.

"We talked it through," Jake adds, "and we decided we're not going to let this take over our lives."

And that is just how they've handled this big shadow. Bill started back on chemotherapy, but not long ago the couple returned from Detroit where Bill fulfilled a longtime dream and was elected to a two-year term as director of Lions Clubs International.

He admits the experience was a little tiring, but he managed to campaign from 5 a.m. to midnight most days! Bill and Jake's three grown children and spouses joined them in Detroit and celebrated together when their dad's election became official.

The family plans to meet in New Orleans and ride the Delta Queen paddleboat together when Bill completes his two-year term. Bill also scheduled speaking engagements as a Lions' director for at least eight states, as well as Canada, India, and Hong Kong—where he really hopes he can take a quick excursion to China and walk a little of the Great Wall.

And beyond the Great Wall, Bill has an even higher goal: to be alive in 2007 and see his wife cancer-free at her five-year mark.

That's how my friend Bill has faced living under the shadow of cancer—by seeing the disease as a curve in the road rather than a blockade.

"I'm conscious that I have it, but I don't worry about it," he says. "Although I know what's going on inside, I'm feeling well. I'm very fortunate because I have an agenda each day."

"We're very busy and we don't have time to think about it," Jake adds.

Bill acknowledges that the recurrence of the cancer has been harder to deal with than the initial diagnosis.

"You keep thinking and praying that the next treatment's going to work," he says. "If it doesn't, I look forward to a new treatment rather than concentrating on the old treatment not working."

He copes with these ups and downs by having faith in his doctor and by constant prayer.

"We don't wear our faith on our sleeves," he says, "but I trust that God is going to give me the ability to handle this new challenge. I don't actually pray so much for [my cancer] to be healed as I pray for the other people [I know with cancer] to be given some peace and comfort as they deal with their own cancer."

The bottom line is that Bill and Jake have no regrets about the decision they've made to pursue life and their dreams to the fullest in spite of cancer's shadow.

"Regardless of what happens, we've made the right decision," Bill says.

Actually, they do have one regret: "We wish we hadn't canceled the trip to Portland when we first found out the cancer was back," he says. "We realize now we could have done it, and I hear I missed a great barbecue salmon dinner!"

      @@   @@   @@

While Bill is a survivor who's often too busy to think about cancer, my friend Genie is very cognizant of her disease—in fact she's lived with it so long she's decided to "make friends" with it.

Now don't get too excited—Genie's not advocating creating a comfortable home for this terrible disease, but for many people nowadays, cancer has become a chronic condition—something more akin to diabetes that people learn to live with for years. Even if your cancer is gone, never to return, I think you'll still appreciate Genie's great attitude, which has helped her cope as a survivor for the past seven years.

You have to know a little about Genie to understand how she came to terms with cancer. The dark-haired, dimpled woman is a native of Puerto Rico where she met the love of her life, a Navy man named Art whom she married and moved with to the United States. They enjoyed decades of marriage before he was diagnosed with a rare blood disorder some fifteen years after successful treatment for bladder cancer. Then in May 1997 Genie was diagnosed with non-Hodgkin's lymphoma and underwent chemotherapy.

Genie's disease was in and out of remission until the fall of 2001 when Art's syndrome went into its final stage at nearly the same time her lymphoma returned. In fact, she had to beg to be discharged from a Maryland hospital where she was receiving in-patient chemo so that she could go home and be with her husband.

Art managed to hang on until Genie arrived, and they had one last day to savor their nearly half century of love.

But there was little if any time for self-pity as Genie faced her own cancer battle. She switched her treatments from Maryland to our office so she would be closer to home. I remember the cold December morning when she first came for a consult. I usually don't come in before eight or eight thirty, but I was worried about this new widow. We met in the parking lot just before seven and watched the sunrise together for a few brief, glorious moments before she headed into the office and the jolting reality of scheduling more chemo.

That December sunrise morning was nearly three years ago, and Genie has had several rounds of chemo and monoclonal antibodies (nonchemo treatments that target only the tumor) since then. Both she and Marc are amazed that her cancer has gone into remission several times, once for an entire year.

One day at our morning support group I asked her how she was coping with her ever-present illness. That's when she introduced me to her "friends."

"This is El Niño," she said in her thick Puerto Rican accent while tapping her left shoulder blade where one tumor is located. "And this is La Niña," she said while gently patting her left side where her second mass is. "That's my little boy and that's my little girl. I named them because they are parts of my body and I think of them as my little babies."

Genie's approach gives new meaning to the phrase "if you can't beat them, join them," doesn't it?

At seventy she relishes being a survivor, and she continues to be active in her church, her community, and with her grandchildren and friends. She recently traveled to Florida and hopes to return again soon.

Don't let her "friendship" with her tumors fool you. "I don't let the cancer win the fight each day," Genie says. "I have a lot of faith and think positive and don't let the cancer get me down."

One of the best things to help her deal with constantly living in cancer's shadow is our support group, she says.

"My advice for those living with chronic cancer is to join a support group and talk about it," she says. "It really helps a lot."

    ☙   ☙   ☙

Now you know how some of my friends are living as survivors: They're volunteering to help others; they're singing new songs; they're taking risks; they're making plans; they're making peace with their circumstances. You can too.

There *is* life after cancer.
(There's even life *with* cancer!)
Life is meant to be savored.

Congratulations! You've survived a cancer diagnosis and treatment for it. God obviously has plans for your life, or you wouldn't still be here. Ask Him to shine His light on your path and then don't be afraid to follow where He leads.

CHAPTER 2

Is Everyone as Paranoid as I Am?

TOP 10 SIGNS YOU'RE PARANOID ABOUT CANCER

10. You have your oncologist's number on speed dial.

9. Your oncologist's secretary has put a call block on your phone number.

8. Ten years after your cancer treatment, your Mediport catheter is still in place "just in case."

7. You take a portable radon detector with you on vacation.

6. You include those little Hemoccult test kits for hidden stool blood with your Christmas cards.

5. You take weekly photos of your moles.

4. You offer to take weekly photos of your friends' moles.

3. You read the obituaries daily to see which ones suggest that "donations may be made to the American Cancer Society."

2. You wear SPF-30 sunscreen . . . indoors when you are sitting by a window.

1. You have a framed copy of the "Seven Warning Signs of Cancer" hanging next to the Ten Commandments on your living-room wall.

I read these reasons to my husband and he didn't even laugh. He didn't get them. But whenever I read them to a roomful of cancer survivors, people always laugh or nod their heads in agreement. Not only are we part of a select group called cancer survivors, we now have an unwanted membership in Club Paranoia.

I would love to quit this club completely, but even after so many years I must admit that I am still much more paranoid about cancer than I ever was before I was first diagnosed. So if you want the really quick, simple answer to the question, "Is everyone as paranoid as I am?" the answer is YES!

The question of why and what to do about it is a little more complicated.

One reason cancer survivors are so paranoid is because once our bodies have betrayed us, it's hard to trust them again. When I was diagnosed with cancer, I looked fine and felt fine. I certainly couldn't imagine I had a life-threatening illness. I thought that people with cancer would look sick or at least feel sick.

My theory in life used to be: If you're not bleeding profusely or in terrible pain, you're okay. My parents, especially my father, who coached sports, always told me to "shake it off" if I got hurt as a child. And that's what I continued to do as an adult.

So I have a little occasional blood in the stool. Probably an old hemorrhoid. I feel fine. Shake it off, I told myself.

So my bowels are occasionally a little different. Probably something I ate. I look fine. Shake it off.

And that's what I did . . . for a year and a half. Both my doctor (make that ex-doctor) and I ignored symptoms that I now know suggest cancer.

Perhaps you did the same. You ignored a warning sign or your doctor didn't seem too concerned about it, so you didn't bother with

any tests. And now that you've finished treatment you want to make
sure you never make that mistake again.

Welcome to Club Paranoia.

This is the place where you feel nervous ignoring things that you
never would have worried about before.

Where a dull headache might be a brain tumor.

Where a tiny, old age spot could be melanoma.

Where indigestion is possibly stomach cancer.

Where a backache surely is bone metastases.

Where lumps, bumps, aches, and pains seem much more
    pronounced right before your next checkup and much less
    right afterward!

Right now I have a little mole on my shin, which looks nothing
like any picture of skin cancer I've seen (and believe me, I've compared it to all of them). I've shown it to two physicians and an
oncology nurse—all of whom have told me it does not look suspicious. Still I have made an appointment with a dermatologist to have
it removed because it appeared suddenly and makes me nervous.
(It doesn't help that my neighbor Sharon, much younger than I am,
had a little mole on her leg, which also didn't look suspicious but
turned out to be melanoma!)

Unless you were a hypochondriac before the cancer diagnosis,
you're probably going to be a little more paranoid about the disease
now. I have yet to meet a survivor who doesn't admit to at least some
degree of irrational fear.

       ☺   ☺   ☺

My friend Jan is one of those admittedly paranoid survivors. It has
been four years since she was diagnosed at age forty-seven with a

large breast tumor, which was attached to the chest wall and difficult
to remove.

Before that fateful day, Jan says she never gave cancer a second
thought.

"I never had that fear of cancer," she explains. "There's no history
of breast cancer in my family and I thought, *It'll never happen to me.*"

That all changed the moment she looked into her family doctor's
face in August 2000.

She had had a "suspicious" mammogram followed by a needle
biopsy and was at her physician's office for the results. Even before
he spoke, she knew it was cancer.

"He had that look on his face that tells you it doesn't look good,"
she remembers.

After Jan recovered from the initial shock, she fought back
through surgery, radiation, and chemo. Follow-up tests continue
to show her to be cancer-free.

"But I am more paranoid," she confesses. "I try not to worry
about it and let it consume me, but the thought is there that it might
come back."

When her arthritis acts up or her back begins to ache, she says
she tries "not to immediately think the cancer's back." Instead she
ignores the physical problem for a while to see if it disappears on its
own. If it persists, she mentions it to one of the physicians following
her care.

Even then she has to decide how aggressive to be in pursuing the
cause of her aches and pains. Recently she visited her family doctor
and mentioned she had a pain in her right hip that extended down
her leg.

"My doctor instantly sent me for a bone scan," Jan recalls.

It turned out to be negative, but she felt better having it done because she knows if the breast cancer recurs it could go to her bones.

On a later visit with the same doctor, she mentioned a recurring problem with headaches and he suggested a CT scan of the brain.

"I declined," Jan says. "I had headaches long before I ever was diagnosed with cancer and I just felt he was being overly cautious."

@@ @@ @@

My goal is not to give you medical advice about when or when not to have diagnostic tests done, but I do like Jan's way of dealing with potential paranoia. She pays attention to her body, notes any changes, brings them to a physician's attention if they don't disappear quickly, and then takes an active role in deciding how to discover their root cause.

Sometimes I think it helps to discuss possible tests with more than one physician. One of the physicians who follows me yearly tends to be very cautious and wants to run tests quickly if a problem surfaces. Another doctor who also follows me prefers watchful waiting and running tests less frequently. Their "votes" sometimes cancel each other out when decisions must be made about my follow-up, so I listen to both sides and cast the deciding vote myself.

A few years ago my blood work came back showing an ovarian tumor marker had more than doubled and was elevated well beyond the normal range, which could signal the presence of ovarian cancer. The first doctor wanted to refer me to a specialist at a nearby major medical center. The other doctor suggested we run the marker again. I went with the latter opinion; the marker came back within the normal range and stayed there during subsequent tests.

I'm not saying I made the *only* right decision and that to seek a second opinion would have been wrong. But I believe I made the right decision for me—one that enabled me to deal successfully with the paranoia of cancer.

Jan and I agree that as time goes on it becomes easier not to be as paranoid. The first couple of years after diagnosis seem to be the hardest. "It gets a lot easier going for checkups after the first two years," Jan says. "I don't get quite as cranky around that time. I used to get really uptight. I'm letting go of it more and more."

One of the ways she does that is by not allowing herself what she calls "negative self-talk."

"I think of myself as cured and not someone waiting to see if the cancer is coming back," she says adamantly. "I do feel like I'm cured even though no doctor ever used those words."

I remember early on wanting a doctor to pronounce me as cured. The surgeon said he got it all, which means *all* that he could see and feel. The oncologist said the chemotherapy decreased my chances of a recurrence. The gastroenterologist said my colon was tumor- and polyp-free. But that was all they said.

I kept waiting for somebody to say I was *cured*, but it never happened. Because there was no medical evidence of any cancer in me, I decided that was all I needed. I decided I didn't want to think of myself as being "in remission" because that sounded as if the cancer was on the verge of coming back. So I solved the problem many, many years ago by telling myself: "You are cured!" (I must admit I would have preferred that the person telling me this good news was wearing a white coat, but that didn't seem likely to happen, so I told myself.)

When patients in Marc's office finish treatment and all visible signs of their cancer are gone, they often ask me: "What do I say to people who ask me if I'm cured?"

I tell them: "I would say you are cured unless somebody proves otherwise."

I would say the same to you: If all visible signs of the cancer are gone, you may tell yourself you are cured unless someone proves otherwise!

And if your cancer is not completely gone but is in remission, I hope you think of yourself as a survivor and not a person waiting to see when the remission will end!

Several years ago a woman attended our support group after being diagnosed with a kind of cancer that can go into remission but is not considered medically curable. She felt quite well and was able to keep a fairly normal routine, but at every meeting she introduced herself as having "terminal cancer."

She thought of herself as dying from cancer instead of living with it. You could just about see the dark shadow of cancer around her as she willingly wrapped herself in its cloak each time she pronounced herself as terminal.

In contrast, Ruth, who attends our evening support group, has been fighting cancer for more than twelve years. A petite woman in her seventies, Ruth has been in and out of remission and her cancer has been considered medically incurable *since* it was diagnosed.

She never would think of introducing herself by saying she has terminal cancer. Instead, she's too busy telling us about her latest trip to Walt Disney World or what she won playing bingo the past week.

"I don't have time to sit around and feel sorry for myself," Ruth says.

Whenever I meet cancer patients who sadly tell me they are terminal, I gently remind them that *life* is terminal.

Besides, I know many patients with "terminal" cancer who have outlived family members who thought they were the healthy ones because they didn't have cancer.

@@   @@   @@

My friend Linda's first bout with cancer in 1991 at the age of forty-three didn't leave her particularly paranoid, but a new diagnosis of an esophageal cancer in 2003 has been more difficult.

"I was really thrown by my second diagnosis [of cancer]," she says. "The first time with the breast cancer I was raising two small children on my own, going to grad school, and teaching, so I was so busy I didn't have time to think about it."

Being diagnosed with another cancer after only four years of marriage to her second husband was more difficult for her emotionally, especially because, unlike her breast cancer, esophageal cancer cannot be easily treated if it recurs.

"They're telling me if it comes back, that's pretty much it," Linda explains.

She's been cancer-free for more than a year now, back to a regular diet, not missing all the extra pounds she shed, but noticing that it's hard to ignore those little aches and pains.

"About five months after my treatments I got this strange sensation in my rib and I thought, *It's got to be the cancer,*" she recalls.

She wasn't due for a checkup with Marc for another month but had the appointment moved up so he could check out the rib pain.

"Everything turned out to be fine," she says. "I kept telling myself that I didn't have anything to worry about, but I was still worried."

Another thing that concerned Linda after her treatments was the fact that Marc "only" wanted to see her for follow-up appointments every six months. After her breast cancer surgery and radiation, an oncologist checked her every other month for a year, then every three months the second year, and finally every six months after that until she reached the five-year mark.

When Marc told her things had changed in medicine and follow-ups were no longer recommended as frequently, that made her a little nervous.

"I remember wishing they were still doing it the other way because it was more of a constant reassurance," she says.

I know exactly what she means.

My chemo treatments were weekly for six months, and when I finished and started coming back once every three months for checkups, I was very nervous. I remember feeling as if I were tiptoeing on a tightrope and somebody had pulled out the safety net from beneath me.

> Who is going to look at every one of my new bumps and lumps each week?
> Who is going tell me that all the weird symptoms I'm having are okay to ignore?
> Who is going to help keep my paranoia in check?
> Where is my safety net?

After a while Marc suggested I come in every six months instead of every three.

"Couldn't I still come every three months?" I pleaded with him as he looked at me incredulously.

I'm sure he thought I would be happy not to have to come in as often, but I was so paranoid about the cancer I felt was lurking around every corner that I needed the constant assurance from my blood work and exams that everything was okay.

I was surprised at my own feelings, as no one ever warned me that the emotional struggles of cancer often are more difficult following treatment than during it. When you're in treatment, you feel as if you're fighting back, conquering the cancer. When the treatment stops, you may feel as if the "enemy" is going to get stronger because you're leaving the battlefield.

That's when it's time to form a new battle plan.

I am not going to tell you what's the best plan for you, but I will tell you to figure one out and stick to it so you don't feel as if you're floundering and cancer can attack you easily again.

Because I felt better getting more frequent checkups with doctors, I scheduled my follow-ups in such a way that someone with MD after his or her name saw me every four months. I saw my oncologist in the late spring, my gynecologist in the early fall, and my gastroenterologist in midwinter. That plan made me feel as if the enemy wouldn't be quite as likely to sneak up on me.

But that plan might make you feel worse—as if you have to see doctors all year long. I know some survivors who like to schedule all their follow-up appointments right around the same time so they can get all the tests—along with the waiting and wondering—over with so they don't have to think about it for another year. They enjoy getting one clean bill of health and not having to think about frequent checkups. Talk to your physicians and come up with a plan that's medically prudent and paranoia-preventing for you!

I truly believe a little paranoia can be healthy because it keeps us on our toes and makes us pay attention to our bodies and the possible warning signs of a recurrence. But most paranoia becomes very unhealthy, negative self-talk.

When I asked my friend Jan how it feels to live with the knowledge that there's a fifty-fifty chance her cancer will return, she says, "I refuse to live in the shadow of cancer. Every day I tell myself I'm a survivor. I know it could come back but I refuse to let it take away the joy of living now."

Linda echoes those sentiments: "I don't think about cancer every day, and it's not a huge shadow in my life."

I'm so glad both of these women aren't frequenting Club Paranoia as often.

❧   ❧   ❧

I used to be an extremely optimistic person, and right up until the time I was diagnosed with cancer, I was *sure* I was fine! That's why every time I face a medical test or procedure today it's hard to convince myself that everything's going to be okay.

> Remember you thought you were fine before, but you weren't—you had cancer.
> Remember you felt fine before, but you weren't—you were in big trouble.
> Remember you looked fine before, but you weren't—you had advanced cancer.

After you've had bad news once (or twice or three times), it's hard not to expect to get it every time. There's often a vague sense that some unseen thing is out to get ahold of you.

I would be a charlatan if I promised you that cancer won't strike you or your loved one again. While I do believe there are things we can do physically, mentally, and spiritually to keep healthy, it is not always possible to prevent cancer from coming back or a new one from forming.

But I also would not be completely honest if I neglected to tell you there is an unseen Someone whose presence we can't escape and who does want to get ahold of us and never let us go.

This Someone knows every paranoid thought before it even crosses our lips and not only sees our future but also holds it in His hands.

You know when I sit down or stand up.
You know my thoughts even when I'm far away.
You see me when I travel and when I rest at home.
You know everything I do.
You know what I am going to say
even before I say it, LORD.
You go before me and follow me.
You place your hand of blessing on my head.
Such knowledge is too wonderful for me,
too great for me to understand!
I can never escape from your Spirit!
I can never get away from your presence!
PSALM 139:2-7

Webster's defines being paranoid as living a life characterized by "irrational suspiciousness and distrustfulness."[3] The above verses are my prescription for that kind of paranoia. When I read them I am reminded that:

Cancer is not everywhere, but God is.
I can get away from cancer, but I can't hide from God.
Tomorrow shouldn't be feared because God is already there.
There is no darkness when I'm in God's presence.

I think cancer survivors and their loved ones should be suspicious of and distrustful of the Big C. It is a very sneaky disease, and we are wise to remain vigilant and not let our guard down when it comes to our health. That makes us smart, not paranoid.

It's the irrational fears we need to avoid. And we do that by being rational—by telling ourselves the truth about our fears.

Most headaches are not brain tumors.

Most breast lumps are not malignant.

Most backaches are not cancer in our bones.

Most of the people diagnosed with cancer today can expect
    to be alive five years from now.[4]

Most cancer survivors are at least a little paranoid, and you're
    not crazy if you are too!

The truth is that while cancer cannot be trusted, God can.

Trust in the LORD with all your heart;
    do not depend on your own understanding.
    PROVERBS 3:5

Let us hold tightly without wavering to the hope we affirm,
for God can be trusted to keep his promise.
    HEBREWS 10:23

I prayed to the LORD, and he answered me,
    freeing me from all my fears. . . .
I cried out to the LORD in my suffering, and he heard me.
    He set me free from all my fears.
    PSALM 34:4, 6 (NLT-1)

I trust in God, so why should I be afraid?
    What can mere mortals do to me?
    PSALM 56:4

You may not be able to completely cancel your membership in Club Paranoia, but you don't have to be a card-carrying member every day!

(By the way, remember that little mole on my shin? The dermatologist removed it and $184 later I found out it was not cancer. Did I mention that paranoia can be very expensive?)

CHAPTER 3

How Do I Turn Off That Voice of Fear?

Fear is a funny thing. Not funny, ha-ha, but funny, peculiar. You need a certain amount of it in order to live safely, but if you have too much of it, it paralyzes you from really living.

Even though it's certainly not the most terrible disease on the face of the earth, cancer has a bad reputation that seems to strike a chord of fear in most families. Some new patients I meet are pretty fearful; others seem to be doing okay but their spouse or kids are afraid.

Sometimes everybody does pretty well all through the treatments and only afterward does that little voice of fear begin to surface. For some it can be a constant, annoying whisper, but most of us find that it gets really loud around checkups. Living as a cancer survivor since 1990 and counseling hundreds of other cancer survivors, I've come to believe that the voice of fear is usually associated with untruths we believe about our diagnosis and prognosis.

I've learned, for instance, that you can't always take a doctor's prediction as absolute fact. If you read my first book, you met my friend Guy who was diagnosed with "incurable" prostate cancer in 1993. He is still alive and cancer-free. So is Melissa, whom doctors said wouldn't make it through the night in February 1996. So is our chemotherapy nurse, Anne, who was given a 10 percent chance of surviving small-cell lung cancer in 1994. In fact, I have three more lung cancer survivors in my little support group—all several years past their treatment and still cancer-free.

Our group even has two brain tumor survivors who remain cancer-free: Chris (whom you'll meet in chapter 4) just celebrated five years cancer-free from a grade III anaplastic astrocytoma and Sherry, who has lived more than twelve years cancer-free since she had the same diagnosis. None of these people were expected to survive cancer but the truth is, they have.

I'm glad doctors no longer keep information from patients as they did decades ago when cancer was spoken about only in hushed tones, and family members knew about the diagnosis but the diagnosed one often didn't.

It's important to realize that the *medical* truth about a cancer diagnosis and prognosis is just one part of the truth about the situation. I believe there are *spiritual truths* that need to be brought into the equation if we cancer survivors are going to really know the whole truth and have the complete picture.

    ☙❧   ❧   ❧

Because doctors had been trying to track down the source of my friend Peggy's physical symptoms for more than a year, she was living with a voice of fear even before she was given a cancer diagnosis.

Peggy, a beautiful gray-eyed blonde, remembers her diagnosis day well. She had seen different doctors and undergone tests for nearly a year and a half before a diagnosis was made. When the final pathology report was ready, she agreed that her gynecologist-oncologist would call her with the results rather than have his office call to make an appointment for her to go in.

"You already know if the doctor wants you to come in [to the office] that it's bad news," she explains.

So in February 2004 at age thirty-nine, Peggy learned from her doctor over the phone that she had a rare form of cervical cancer. "In that moment it was as if my body answered the call," she says, "and it was shaking, literally shaking. At one point I had to ask [the doctor] to stop [talking] so I could breathe. The word *cancer* hit my ear and vibrated down to my toes," she says.

That phone call impressed upon Peggy, a first-grade reading specialist, the power of words.

"I realized how powerful words were, and if those words could bring me to my knees, I wondered what other words could make me stand back up," she recalls.

And that's when Peggy began an incredible journey—a journey to find words of life rather than words of death through her cancer experience.

Peggy acknowledges that she had feared cancer in her own life for some time as she had watched it strike those she loved: her grandfather, her husband's aunt, and even her dog. She didn't want the Big C to strike her, so the petite woman tried to take good care of herself and carefully watched what she ate.

"I wasn't obsessed with cancer, but I had thought about it and whether I thought I could ever handle it," she says.

To those around her, Peggy appeared to be cool, calm, and collected, but inside she was "fearful of many things."

"I looked on the outside as absolutely in control, but I was a worrier and a fearful person," she explains.

Peggy and I met shortly before her surgery in March 2004 when she attended my evening Cancer Prayer Support Group after she had read a copy of my first book. I remember the meeting well because it was a huge group (for us) of twenty-three people, including three first-timers. As the lone facilitator, I knew it would be a challenge to keep the meeting flowing smoothly.

I did my best but things did not go well: One of the newcomers talked way too long during his introduction, telling us details of every operation he had ever had and refusing to take a breath so I could politely jump in. He then proceeded to ask people personal questions and suggest ways I could run the group better.

I had a headache before we were halfway around the table with introductions. Afterward I told my husband that it was the worst support group meeting I had ever facilitated.

But Peggy remembers the meeting very differently.

"I came to the support group meeting wanting to hear everybody's story of how they empowered themselves to beat cancer," she says. "I still wanted to be in control of the cancer, and I thought that somebody in the group was going to give me the answer, give me the cure.

"But as I looked around that table, I saw faces of faith. I saw that faith in God was what was getting people through cancer. I saw people laughing and living because they had faith."

At the "worst" support group meeting on record, Peggy told me she found the cure for what was missing in her life: a relationship with the living God.

Don't you just love how God can use us in spite of us? I left that meeting feeling like a failure as a facilitator (and if a videotape existed I think it would back me up!), but God didn't need a perfectly run meeting to touch Peggy. He simply needed a heart seeking the truth.

"I always believed in God," Peggy says. "I saw Him work in other people's lives and kind of acknowledged Him but not in any personal way. I trusted other people's faith because I didn't have any of my own. I used to ask other people to pray for me because I didn't think God would answer my prayers."

After attending our group, Peggy said she decided to pray on her own: "'Lord, You need to carry this cancer—it's too big for me.' And that's when I surrendered the cancer to Him," she says.

A few days later, a conversation about faith with a Christian physician made her realize God wanted something more from her, so she prayed again: "God, You want more than my illness. You want my whole life."

"And that's when I surrendered everything," she says with a smile. She began reading her Bible and attending worship with a friend. She also joined a small group meeting at my house to study Rick Warren's best seller, *The Purpose-Driven Life*. As she did, Peggy began to realize that the fears in her life stemmed from many untruths she believed about herself, her past, and her future.

"I never believed in Satan before, but after reading the Bible I realized there is a true devil and he has told me lies for many years in my life," she explains. "I realized Satan lies about God, people around me, and me. It's like he's a little voice of fear on my shoulder."

You may have heard that little voice too.

The cancer's going to come back.

Nobody survives this kind of cancer.

Maybe the surgeon didn't really get it all.

Don't make too many plans because you might not be here.

Peggy says when she hears that voice she puts her index finger and thumb together and "I flick it right off my shoulder!" She also stops that voice from speaking up so loudly and so often by filling her mind with truth from God's Word.

Proverbs 4:20-23 has become a real favorite:

My child, pay attention to what I say.
   Listen carefully to my words.
Don't lose sight of them.
   Let them penetrate deep into your heart,
for they bring life to those who find them,
   and healing to their whole body.
Guard your heart above all else,
   for it determines the course of your life.

As cancer survivors, we need to tell ourselves the truth about our circumstances.

We had cancer.

We may get it again.

We may not get it again.

Life is always terminal; cancer may or may not be.

That's really all we know for sure. Despite researchers' statistics and doctors' prognoses, anything else is pure speculation.

    ❧   ❧   ❧

I'm reading the book *Telling Yourself the Truth* by psychologist Dr. William Backus and psychotherapist Marie Chapian, which says— just as Peggy has surmised—that most of people's fear, depression, anxiety, and anger stems from misbeliefs about themselves or their situation.

The authors explain that misbeliefs usually appear to be true to the person repeating them. Often they do have an element of truth in them, but the bottom line is that they are based on erroneous assumptions.

One misbelief I had when I was diagnosed with cancer caused me a great deal of fear: *Ralph's first wife died even though people prayed for her. God didn't heal her and He's not going to heal me.*

The truth about my situation was that my husband's first wife did indeed die from Lou Gehrig's disease despite much prayer for her healing. The lie was that because of her circumstance, prayers for my healing would not be effective and I would die too.

Maybe your misbelief is something similar:

My mother died from this kind of cancer and I will too.
My neighbor's cancer came back and mine will too.

Or how about one of these:

I am no longer beautiful without my breast.
I can't live life with a colostomy.
I am less of a man without my sexual function.

Or maybe even this popular myth:

I have to think positive because negative thinking will cause
    a recurrence.

Can you see the misbeliefs in your life? What are the half-truths behind that voice of fear?

Identifying and calling them by name is the first step in turning off the voice.

Telling yourself the truth about the situation is the next step. "In emotional and mental health what you believe is *all important.* It makes a difference what you believe. Other people, circumstances, events and material things are *not* what make you happy. What you *believe* about these things makes you happy or unhappy," Backus and Chapian write.[5]

I love watching and listening to those with medically incurable cancer who attend my support group but still find much happiness. Because of their circumstances, others might say these people have the right to be fairly fearful. But these survivors have come to realize—as have those of us who are cured—that we don't need the right circumstances to be happy, but we do need to *believe* the right things about our circumstances to be happy.

When I finished treatment for my cancer, the odds the cancer would come back were *greater* than the odds it wouldn't. That doesn't sound like a situation that would make a person very happy. But what I believed about my circumstances did give me joy.

I believed the truth that I was already a cancer survivor: "For as he thinks within himself, so he is" (Proverbs 23:7, NASB).

And I believed the truth that nothing, including cancer and its treatment, can separate me from God's great love for me: "And I am convinced that nothing can ever separate us from God's love. Neither death nor life, neither angels nor demons, neither our fears for today nor our worries about tomorrow—not even the powers of hell can separate us from God's love" (Romans 8:38).

I also believed the truth that God didn't need good odds to heal me, that there are people everywhere surviving despite their odds: "For nothing is impossible with God" (Luke 1:37).

These truths and many others helped me turn down the volume of that voice of fear when I was first diagnosed, and they continue to help keep it down as I live in cancer's shadow.

Peggy says she tries to fill her mind with truth by reading the Bible every day, memorizing helpful verses, and talking about Scriptures with others.

What's feeding your mind these days? Is it the obituaries as you look to see if anyone you know has died? Is it news of the latest celebrity who has cancer? Or is it the awesome truth that God really does love you and that His plans for your life are always good?

Is your mind filled with the truth that the God who created this universe by simply speaking words is a lot more powerful than any possible misguided cells within our bodies and a lot more trustworthy than any statistics in a medical journal? Or are you listening to misbeliefs, those half-truths racing through your head?

I believe that one way to find the light in cancer's shadow is to compare God's truth to each and every detail of our circumstances. What are you believing about your past, present, or future that isn't absolutely 100 percent true? Jesus promised His followers: "And you will know the truth, and the truth will set you free" (John 8:32).

I really enjoy the television show *CSI: Crime Scene Investigation*, which depicts forensic investigators searching for clues to solve murders (though I have to close my eyes on all the close-up gory parts). The CSIs always are shining their flashlights in every nook and cranny, trying to turn up clues that might have been missed. And sure enough, they always find something.

That's the way I picture us cancer survivors: With our flashlights, we look around the corners of our minds for any thoughts that are making us fearful, discouraged, worried, anxious, or depressed. When we find them, we don't put them under the microscope, but we do hold them up to the truth and see if they are genuine or whether they are misbeliefs. We throw away all the misbeliefs and replace them with the truth.

I believe that when we live by the truth of God's Word and His ways, we can fully live again.

Your word is a lamp for my feet
     and a light for my path.
I've promised it once, and I'll promise again:
     I will obey your wonderful laws.
I have suffered much, O LORD;
     restore my life again, just as you promised.
PSALM 119:105-107 (NLT-1)

You, too, can turn off that little voice of fear by telling yourself the truth about cancer and about your life after a cancer diagnosis.

I'd like to suggest, though, that there's one voice of fear that you should turn *on* if it isn't already. Remember how we said that some fears are lifesaving? Well, this is a lifesaving, life-giving fear.

It's the fear of the Lord.

It's not a "fall down and shake because you're afraid of getting zapped" kind of fear. Instead it's a *Wow!* kind of fear—the kind where you are just in awe and amazement and wonder and reverence about God because of what He has done and still can do.

It's this "fear" that Peggy and I have discovered reduces all the other fears.

I love how Psalm 112 describes these "fear-filled" kind of people:

Happy are those who fear the LORD.
Yes, happy are those who delight in doing what he commands. . . .
When darkness overtakes the godly, light will come bursting in.
     They are generous, compassionate, and righteous. . . .
They do not fear bad news;
     they confidently trust the LORD to care for them.
They are confident and fearless
     and can face their foes triumphantly.
PSALM 112:1, 4, 7-8 (NLT-1)

The Old Testament prophet Isaiah explained how he, too, learned to have the right kind of fear after God warned him that his country would be invaded.

> *The LORD has said to me in the strongest terms: "Do not think like everyone else does. Do not be afraid that some plan conceived behind closed doors will be the end of you. Do not fear anything except the LORD Almighty. He alone is the Holy One. If you fear him, you need fear nothing else. He will keep you safe."*
>
> ISAIAH 8:11-14 (NLT-1)

I don't know about you, but that's one voice of fear I always want to hear.

CHAPTER 4

Do I Have to Go to Oz to Get Some Courage?

If someone had said to me in May 1990, "Next month you are going to be diagnosed with metastatic cancer, have major surgery, and then need a year of chemotherapy," I would have responded, "No way! I cannot possibly go through that!"

I am by nature a wimp.

I bruise and scar easily. Loud noises hurt my ears. I get motion sickness just turning around in the front seat of a car.

And I definitely do not like pain.

When I made the appointment for my first postcancer colonoscopy (definitely not scheduled to air on national TV like Katie Couric's!), I told the secretary I wanted plenty of anesthesia because I had been uncomfortably awake during most of the procedure the first time with a different physician.

"Be sure and tell the doctor," I instructed her. But her casual "uh-huh" left me feeling that she didn't think it was a real priority.

"Write on my chart 'Wimp—needs lots of anesthesia,'" I instructed her again. She laughed and I still wondered whether she knew how serious I was.

My question was answered a few weeks later when I met my new gastroenterologist, Dr. Jim Srour, just moments before he started the procedure. The IV already was running into my hand as he read my

medical chart. "I see it says here that you are a wimp and need lots
of anesthesia," he said without cracking a smile.

"Yes, that's me!" I exclaimed.

He instructed the nurse to put more anesthesia in my IV, and that
is how and why Jim Srour became my favorite gastroenterologist!

Like the Cowardly Lion in *The Wizard of Oz*, I often feel I could
use a dose of courage, but it's not usually as easy as getting a little
more medicine in an IV tube. However, I do believe it is possible,
even if we're not naturally brave, to supernaturally receive courage
for ourselves and even enough to share with others.

☙☙   ☙☙   ☙☙

I'd like you to meet Chris and Jutta (pronounced YOU-tuh), two
close friends in their thirties who are surviving very scary cancer
diagnoses.

Neither woman would call herself courageous, but I think it
takes a great deal of courage to live in the shadow of pancreatic
cancer as Jutta does and in the shadow of brain cancer as Chris
does.

"I'm not the kind of person to go out and do something
that nobody else has ever done," Jutta says. "But I'm always a
go-getter. If you put something on my plate for me to do, I'll do
it 100 percent."

Jutta got a huge surprise on her plate when the thirty-eight-year-
old awoke from exploratory surgery in July 2003 to discover she
wasn't jaundiced because of a drug reaction but because of a small
malignant tumor in her pancreas. Up until that time, Jutta, a wife and
mother of two children, then ten and six, had never even considered
the possibility that she might be seriously ill.

"I felt there was nothing wrong with me," she says. "I just brushed it all off."

But the harsh reality was that she had one of the deadliest kinds of cancer and it already had spread to the lymph nodes. "The day after surgery, the oncologist came up to my room and said, 'You better get your act together. You have cancer and you've only got two years,'" Jutta recalls.

Hearing that she had such a difficult-to-treat cancer was shocking, but even worse, Jutta says, "was the way I was told."

"It took me at least a month to get over that," she adds. Eventually she decided the doctor's prediction was only that—a prediction—and she would not live believing it *had* to come true. Twenty-one months later, she has finished her year of chemotherapy and continues to be cancer-free.

"I don't think his prediction is going to come true," she adds with a smile.

Still, the young mother, who came to this country in 1991 from her native Germany, has been honest with her children about her uncertain future. "You can't hide it from your children," she says. "You can't put it in the closet and not talk about it. Your kids are not dumb and they can tell something's not right."

       ๏ ๏ ๏

I know what a great deal of courage it takes to talk to children about cancer in the family.

When I was diagnosed, our daughters were eight, ten, and twelve, and we wanted to protect them from cancer's assault on me. So we decided we would tell them I was going to have surgery, but we wouldn't use the word *cancer*.

That bright idea lasted about twenty-four hours until I realized that somebody in our church or our community was going to use the word *cancer* and my girls would hear it.

So we sat them down again and, using the dreaded word, tried to give them an idea of what to expect. I remember being careful not to give them too much information that would scare them but also not making promises we couldn't keep.

We were cautious not to talk about any specific cure odds, but about five years later my eldest daughter, Danielle, confessed she had overheard someone talking at church and knew that the odds I would die were greater than the odds I would live.

I wish I had known Danielle knew that because I would have talked more with her about my uncertain future and encouraged her more to ask questions and express worries. But she is my introvert, and she didn't mention the overheard conversation until she was seventeen.

Both Jutta and I agree that for us the scariest part about cancer was not what might happen to us, but what would happen to our children *without* us.

Still, Jutta says she summoned the courage to tell her older child the truth. "God has poured courage into me to show [my children] that faith in God is the right way to handle this," she says. "I told my daughter that there's a chance I might die; that I might not make it. She said, 'It's all right, Mommy, because I know where you'll be.'"

@@   @@   @@

If you still have children at home—or even grandchildren nearby—you have a great opportunity to show them your faith in action. It's easy to talk about things like praying, having faith, and trusting God, but a diagnosis of cancer in the family gives us a chance to see if our walk matches our talk.

In those first really dark days after my diagnosis, I remember feeling as if I wanted to go to bed, pull the covers up over my head, and have somebody call me to come out when it was all over. But I also remember my head talking some courage into my faint heart.

You've always told your children:

> That God can be trusted.
> *Now they can see if you really do trust Him.*

> That God is faithful.
> *Now they can see if you will be too.*

> That knowing Jesus makes all the difference.
> *Now they can see if it really does.*

We were a family, and that "for better or for worse" pledge my husband and I made applied to our children too. Together we would face cancer with the courage that God supernaturally would pour into each of our hearts, no matter what our age or bravery status.

Cancer probably was the best real-life lesson to prove to my kids that God can and will meet our deepest needs—that He can give us courage to face things we never thought we could.

My daughters, now in their twenties and living on their own, also have seen that because God poured courage into our hearts, we now can pour it into others.

> *He comforts us in all our troubles so that we can comfort others.*
> *When others are troubled, we will be able to give them the same*

comfort God has given us. . . . For when God comforts us, it is so
that we, in turn, can be an encouragement to you.
    2 CORINTHIANS 1:4, 6 (NLT-1)

Jutta says she has experienced this firsthand many times since
her diagnosis.

"I've talked with a lot of cancer patients and their family members, and I know it has helped them as they hear my story," she says.
"It encourages them that they can face it too."

Jutta, who still speaks with a rich German accent, believes that
it's important to talk about the feelings of living in cancer's shadow.
"I don't want to swallow it and keep it inside me," she says. "If I talk
about it, it helps others and it helps me."

But Jutta does more than just talk. She is a woman of action.
Since her diagnosis and despite her poor prognosis, she has started
her own home business and continues to volunteer in her church.

"You don't stop living just because you hear that word *cancer*,"
she says. "That's the worst thing you can do.

"I believe that somebody who still sets goals lives longer," she
adds. "Even if my cancer would have been stage IV, I would still have
gone for my goals. One of my goals is that I want to be an encouragement to other people."

One of the people encouraged by Jutta is her friend Chris, who
was diagnosed with brain cancer four years before Jutta received her
diagnosis. The two women were close friends before Jutta's diagnosis
and have become even closer since.

But Chris insists that Jutta is the only courageous one.

"I don't know why you would want to write about me," she told
me when I asked her about telling some of her story. "I'm such a
wimp."

"Because there will be lots of wimps reading this book and they will be glad to read about you!" I assured her.

Besides, I think it takes a lot of courage for Chris to live in the shadow of a brain tumor, wondering about every tension headache, having her head scanned for masses every six months, knowing that she has outlived the vast majority of those with her kind of cancer.

Her family doctor recently told her at her five-year cancer-free checkup: "You shouldn't even be here. I wish I could explain it [but] I can't explain why you're still here."

Like Jutta, Chris woke up from surgery to discover she had a malignant tumor. Her ordeal began in July 1999 when she suffered a grand mal seizure while sleeping beside her husband.

"He thought I fell out of bed," she recalls. "He was trying to get me up, but when he rolled me over I was turning blue."

It took an ambulance crew about half an hour to get to the thirty-six-year-old woman's rural home. She was sent home from the hospital without a diagnosis, but two days later was back again after another seizure.

A subsequent test revealed a golf ball–sized tumor in the right front area of her brain.

"They operated on me on Monday but I don't remember anything of those three days [before]," she says.

"I never knew what the odds were regarding survival," she adds. "No one ever told me that I only had a certain length of time left. If they had, I think I would have panicked." (About 30 percent of brain tumor survivors are still alive five years after their diagnosis according to American Cancer Society statistics.)

Chris, the self-admitted wimp, went through thirty radiation treatments and about nine months of chemotherapy. Doctors wanted to give her a year's worth, but like me, she was allergic to one of the drugs and had her treatments cut short.

While Chris still was undergoing treatment, she and Jutta became friends at a women's Bible study Jutta was leading at their church. Chris, her husband, and their then two-year-old son, only recently had begun to attend the church at the invitation of one of her physicians, who found out they didn't worship anywhere.

"I had so many questions about God and all kinds of spiritual things," recalls Chris, who by nature is very shy and quiet. "I always thought they were stupid so I didn't bring them up [before], but Jutta didn't seem to mind explaining things to me. And she would always give me a hug when I got there and when I left."

A friendship was easily forged between the two women, and Chris's love for God grew alongside her love for Jutta. On the one-year anniversary of her brain surgery, Chris was baptized in a church member's swimming pool with Jutta cheering her on. A couple of months later another church member challenged Chris to start a cancer support group at their church.

"I know I can't lead it" was Chris's noncourageous reply.

But soon another cancer survivor in the congregation volunteered to help her and monthly meetings began.

Jutta recalls that Chris often suggested she come to the group and share the story of her faith in God, but she refused, saying, "I don't have cancer and I don't know what they're all going through."

But then, Jutta got her own up-close-and-personal look at cancer when she received her pancreatic cancer diagnosis about three years later.

"I always prayed that God would use me no matter what," she says.

"If I'd have known it would result in this, I wouldn't have prayed that way," she adds with a laugh.

So Chris got her "wish": Jutta came to her support group and helped pour courage into the hearts of others in cancer's shadow. Chris says Jutta has a real gift of encouragement. "Every time I see her, she's picking me up; she's there comforting me," she explains.

Chris realizes that because she tends to be withdrawn and discouraged, she needs to spend time with people like Jutta who help her feel encouraged and optimistic about her own uncertain future.

"I'm careful who I spend time with," she says. "I do think it's the people you surround yourself with that make the difference."

One of the ways Jutta has noticed that God pours courage into people's hearts is "putting the right people in your life at the right time."

The apostle Paul talks about this method of God's encouragement in a letter he wrote to the believers in Corinth, Greece.

> *When we arrived in Macedonia, there was no rest for us. We faced conflict from every direction, with battles on the outside and fear on the inside. But God, who encourages those who are discouraged, encouraged us by the arrival of Titus. His presence was a joy.*
> 2 CORINTHIANS 7:5-7

Many times I have seen God, who encourages the discouraged, "show up" in just the right person and at just the right time to encourage me. I hope you pray believing He will do the same for you and those you love.

၆၆   ၆၆   ၆၆

I also hope you see that receiving supernatural courage is not the same as being a naturally brave person. It's not something magical that happens to some people and not to others. No, you don't have to go to Oz to find it.

The kind of courage I'm writing about is what God supernaturally pours into our hearts—even into ordinary, wimpy hearts like mine—through the power of His Spirit as we draw close to Him. And when He does, others notice—especially if we're in a difficult situation.

"People tell me that I have a shine about me that they just don't usually see in people," Jutta says. "I tell them that's just a gift from God."

> We now have this light shining in our hearts, but we ourselves
> are like fragile clay jars containing this great treasure. This makes
> it clear that our great power is from God, not from ourselves.
> 2 CORINTHIANS 4:7

Yes, it takes courage to live in cancer's shadow, but it's not something we just have to reach way down deep into ourselves and find. No, instead, it's power we receive from God to be strong even when we are weak.

I believe that courage is not living without fear—it's living in spite of fear.

I love the late psychiatrist M. Scott Peck's thoughts on courage: "The absence of fear is not courage; the absence of fear is some kind of brain damage. Courage is the capacity to go ahead in spite of the fear, or in spite of the pain."[6]

God will give you enough courage to live with an uncertain future. And as you encourage others with your story, you won't have *less* courage; you will feel even *more* encouraged.

I have seen this happen time and again in my job as a patient advocate. People often say to me, "I could never do a job like that."

My reply is, "I can't either, but God can through me. I allow Him to pour courage into me so I have it to pour into others."

So take a new grip with your tired hands and stand firm on your shaky legs. Mark out a straight path for your feet. Then those who follow you, though they are weak and lame, will not stumble and fall but will become strong.

HEBREWS 12:12-13 (NLT-1)

I know it is difficult to persevere in cancer's shadow, but I am convinced that it's not the *amount* of our faith that gives us courage, it's the *object* of our faith that makes all the difference.

Whenever I place my faith in God, I find courage. I don't need luck, natural bravery, or a trip to see the Wizard of Oz! You don't need a lot of faith to find courage, but you do need to place your faith in the only One who can meet your deepest needs.

These things I have spoken to you, so that in Me you may have peace. In the world you have tribulation, but take courage; I have overcome the world.

Jesus speaking in JOHN 16:33 (NASB)

Do not be afraid or discouraged, for the LORD will personally go ahead of you. He will be with you; he will neither fail you nor abandon you.

DEUTERONOMY 31:8

CHAPTER 5

How Do I Keep (or Get) a Sense of Humor?

I read recently that "laughter is like changing a baby's diaper—it doesn't permanently solve any problems, but it does make things more acceptable for a while."

I don't know how long it's been since your or your loved one's cancer diagnosis, but when I was diagnosed with advanced cancer in 1990 I couldn't imagine anything funny about a life-threatening disease.

I still don't believe cancer is humorous, but I have discovered that every time a person facing cancer laughs, it reminds us that we are still alive, and that is a very good thing. I am a firm believer that we all need to keep—or get—a sense of humor as we live in cancer's shadow.

So if you're tired of worrying and would like to laugh a little today, I'd like to introduce you to my friend Dorothy, one of those really great people with the ability to make the most out of life's embarrassing moments even though she has lived in cancer's shadow for many years. I know her funny stories won't permanently solve any problems in your life, but I think it will feel really good at least for a little while to "have your diaper changed"!

I met Dorothy in 1997, four years after she was diagnosed with stage III colon cancer. She was seventy-four, widowed, and still in remission despite an initial poor prognosis because of widespread lymph-node involvement. I only saw her once a year at her recheck visits until November 2000, when the cancer unfortunately recurred and spread.

By this time she was nearly eighty and had enjoyed an unexpected seven and a half years of remission, which made this latest bitter news easier to swallow, she said. Dorothy wasn't the type of patient who was easily discouraged either. In fact, she told me in March 2003 that her surgeon had predicted that she had only three months to live when he operated on her twenty-eight months earlier!

"I feel I still have work to do. Besides, I don't have the sense to give in," she added with a big smile.

And she did not give in. Instead she fought her disease with the help of new chemo, a supportive family, and the healing medicine of laughter. Invariably when she would come into our office, Dorothy would have a hilarious story to share.

I remember the funniest story she ever told was March 21, 2001—I know the exact date because afterward I ran to my office and wrote it down word for word as best I could remember it. I knew I would never want to forget this story.

Dorothy said that after her last treatment she felt a little hungry and decided to drive to a nearby restaurant called Claire's, famous around town for its broasted chicken and fresh peach sundaes. She parked near the door on the side of the restaurant, which had large picture windows for customers to gaze out on the parking lot.

As she stepped out of the car, she felt the elastic in the waistband of her slacks snap. Not wanting her now-too-loose slacks to slide down, she quickly grabbed the waistband with her right hand. As she did, a huge gust of wind came up and—you guessed it—blew her wig right off her bald head.

Of course Dorothy lunged for the wig but it got away. She did, however, manage to set off the car alarm on the keys she still held in her tightly clenched hand, which also was holding up her slacks.

Picture this: the car's lights flashing; the horn honking; the slacks still slipping; and the curly, platinum blonde wig still blowing away as Dorothy, a completely bald, five-foot-nine-inch-tall octogenarian, runs across the parking lot.

"I kept frantically trying to punch buttons on the keys to turn off the alarm, but I didn't want to drop my drawers," she said. "My wig just looked like a little tumbleweed as it rolled across the parking lot."

Finally it came to rest against a truck tire and Dorothy started talking to the wig as she ran closer: "You might as well let me catch you now because if you blow under the truck I'm crawling under there to get you and you won't get away!"

Apparently the wig believed her and stayed put until she could grab it.

She plopped the little tumbleweed back on her head and finally found the right button to turn off her car alarm.

"What did you do then?" I asked when I could get a breath after all the laughter.

"I got in the car, put it in reverse, and drove across town to McDonald's," she said. "I may never go to Claire's again!"

Every time I drive by Claire's, I smile as I picture Dorothy chasing her tumbleweed wig that day. I imagine there are probably some Claire's customers who witnessed the event and still relish retelling the story!

☯   ☯   ☯

One of the amazing things about Dorothy's story is that I really didn't *want* her to tell me the story that day.

You see, I was sitting in the chemo room with another couple who had just gotten bad news about the husband's scan. His wife was fighting tears. Judy, our office manager, came in and said, "Dorothy, did you tell Lynn about your wig?"

I figured it was a funny story and my first thought was: *Oh, no, not now. This couple is too sad to hear this.*

Fortunately I didn't stop Dorothy from telling it right then because when she finished and all the laughter died down in the room, the patient's wife smiled at Dorothy and said: "Thanks, I really needed that."

Judy's timing—actually God's timing—was perfect as those few moments of laughter reminded this sad couple that they still were alive and that felt so good.

The next time I saw Dorothy a few weeks later I jokingly asked, "Any more wig stories?"

"Actually, I did have another problem with it," she said with a mischievous grin.

It seems that this time, she and a female friend were at a funeral for a mutual friend. Afterward they both went to the cemetery for the committal service, and as they walked toward the grave site, it began to rain.

Dorothy's friend was well prepared, and she pulled out an umbrella and popped it up to keep them both dry.

Now remember that I mentioned that Dorothy was very tall? Her friend wasn't nearly as tall, and as she popped up the umbrella, one of the little, round metal spokes caught Dorothy's wig and pulled it up and off her still very bald head!

Dorothy quickly grabbed the wig, got it unhooked, and plunked it back down in its proper place.

Then the real problem began.

Dorothy's friend began to snicker. Then Dorothy began to snicker. Dorothy's friend tried to stifle the laughter welling up inside of her at the thought of her bald friend's wig hanging off her umbrella.

Dorothy's friend began to shake, and Dorothy also started to shake with stifled laughter.

"What did you do?" I asked as I imagined the scene in my mind.

"Well, we covered our mouths and prayed that people would think we were sobbing with grief instead of laughing!" she explained.

It seemed to work as most of the other mourners gave them sympathetic looks.

"Afterward we told our [deceased] friend's husband what had happened and why we were acting like that and he laughed too," Dorothy said.

Dorothy is definitely the *only* patient who disappointed us when her hair grew back!

      ◎   ◎   ◎

About a month before my diagnosis, I was a reporter for a local paper doing a story about the new cancer support group at the local hospital. I interviewed Marc for the story and visited his office. When I walked by the chemo room, I glanced in at all the patients in recliners hooked up to IVs. It was an incredibly scary picture to me. But what was even scarier was that the patients were *laughing.* I remember thinking, *They must not know they have cancer because how can people with cancer laugh?* I went home that day and told my husband, "If I had cancer, I definitely would not be sitting there laughing."

Four weeks later when I was diagnosed with colon cancer, I

definitely was not laughing. When I went for my first chemo treatment in August 1990, I was so frightened I knew I would *never* laugh while hooked up to an IV getting toxic chemicals, which would perhaps give me a 40 percent chance to live.

But that was before I met Marc's head chemo nurse, Ruth, who's been with him since he opened his office in 1989. She definitely has breathed a few too many chemo fumes because she made a not-so-funny experience not so sad. I always enjoyed hearing her jokes and reading her bulletin board filled with humorous signs.

Men have feelings too, but who cares?

I just got a gun for my wife.
It's the best trade I ever made.

Some days you're the pigeon
And some days you're the statue.

Before I knew what had happened, she had me laughing too.

There was still nothing funny about having cancer or getting chemo or not knowing if I would see my daughters grow up, but every time I laughed it felt so good and reminded me that I was still alive.

So I decided I needed to keep my sense of humor and started to look for funny things *in spite* of my serious predicament.

One of the first things my family found to joke about was the new chemo pill I took—Levamisole. It was a newly approved oral medicine, and I was the first patient at Marc's office to take it. I soon learned that in reality it was a worming medicine designed to kill intestinal parasites in sheep and dogs.

Whenever I took a pill, I started barking and chasing my squealing daughters around the house. My husband mentioned to our friends that I had been dewormed and he was thinking of getting me a rabies shot too. The pills were very expensive and my husband often suggested we call the vet to see if we could get them cheaper there.

Another drug I took was fluorouracil, commonly called 5-FU. I was very allergic to 5-FU, and one of the reactions was that my eyes watered profusely. It looked as if I were crying all the time. This was really annoying and depressed me a lot.

So I decided to have some fun with that too. When we went on long trips and I drove, I used my glasses to hold little balls of tissue in the corner of each eye. I left the tissue wads in place when I went through tollbooths and grinned at the toll taker as my children slid down in the backseat from embarrassment.

Those who know me well know that my right eye still tears because the tear duct is permanently scarred. I also have learned to laugh about this. Awhile back a lady in my church told me, "I just love to watch you during worship. You're so touched by everything. I see you crying."

"Really? Did you see me crying during the offering, too?" I asked her.

If you tell me something sad and you think I'm crying with you, make sure you check to see if tears are coming out of my left eye as well as my right.

     ◎   ◎   ◎

Laughter is good for the body. Science is just figuring that out, but the Bible told us so long ago.

A cheerful look brings joy to the heart, and good news gives health to the bones.
PROVERBS 15:30 (NIV)

A cheerful heart is good medicine, but a crushed spirit dries up the bones.

PROVERBS 17:22 (NIV)

Drs. Lee Berk and Stanley Tam of Loma Linda University are some of the leading researchers today on the therapeutic benefits of laughter. Their published studies have shown that laughter has many positive effects on our bodies, including activating our immune system.

It increases the number and activity of some white blood cells called T and B cells, natural killers that fight viral infections and some types of cancer cells. Laughter increases the antibody IgA, which fights upper respiratory tract infections. A hearty chuckle increases gamma interferon, which stimulates various components of the immune system.

Laughing increases our heart rate, and some have likened this to "internal jogging." It's an aerobic activity that works the diaphragm and increases our bodies' ability to use oxygen. That's why after a big laugh you often feel the need to sigh and take a big breath of air. Sure beats thirty minutes on the NordicTrack.

As we laugh, our blood pressure temporarily increases; however, that is followed by a prolonged, mild decrease in blood pressure. Laughter also decreases various hormone levels—the kinds associated with the fight-or-flight response—and makes us feel less stressed, more relaxed. That's why people say things like "I laughed so hard I couldn't get up" or "I laughed so hard I fell over."

I've often heard that laughter increases beta-endorphins, the body's natural painkillers that distance runners often feel. I couldn't find any published data on this so perhaps it's just an urban legend, but I wouldn't be surprised if eventually it is proven true.

I did find a published study in the *Journal of Holistic Nursing*, in which patients were told one-liners after surgery and before pain medication was given. Those exposed to humor rated their pain as less compared to patients who didn't get a dose of laughter.[7] There's no doubt that laughter is a wonderful, free diversion that helps us forget about aches and pains for a while and makes cancer's shadow seem much smaller.

That's one of the reasons the chemo room in our office is such an emotionally healing place to be—we laugh a lot in there. It's hard not to smile when you're getting chemo from a geisha girl and a leprechaun, as patients did just a couple of weeks ago on our annual fall dress-up day. In past years, the nurses have dressed as a fairy godmother, clowns, and the Blues Brothers. One year, two nurses dressed as a farmer and a cow. Of course, Ruth was the black-and-white spotted cow, complete with little plastic udders as she offered to put fresh milk in patients' coffee.

When people finish chemo in our office, they get treated to the "Blue Light Special." The nurses turn on a revolving blue light similar to the kind a popular discount store once used to highlight sales. The patient gets a cardboard, jeweled crown and a big sticker proclaiming "Say NO to drugs!"

Then a parade begins as the nurses carry around our collection of singing, inanimate objects. A bluebird chirps out "Zippity doo dah, zippity ay, my oh my what a wonderful day." Then a little hamster dressed in boxing attire begins pelting the air to the theme of *Rocky*. Finally an eighteen-inch-tall plastic James Brown starts gyrating and crooning, "I feel good; I knew that I would."

Everybody looks forward to getting the royal treatment when they finish treatment!

◎◎   ◎◎   ◎◎

One of the funny things about laughter is that it's always better when it's shared with others. It's easier to have our funny bones tickled when we're with others. Sometimes the people laughing at a joke are funnier than the joke itself! Shared laughter is also one of the reasons my Cancer Prayer Support Group is so popular.

I invited the breast cancer survivor named Ruth whom I mentioned in chapter 2 to my support group for years before she came. She told me: "I can stay home and cry by myself. Why do I want to drive somewhere and cry with a bunch of other cancer patients?"

I finally convinced Ruth to come just once. She couldn't believe how much we laughed together. Now she's a regular and believes it's definitely worth the drive to *laugh* with a bunch of cancer patients!

The support group I lead has a reputation for loud laughter. When the group meets in the evening at our church, people frequently gather for other meetings throughout the building. As they hear raucous laughter coming from our room, they often ask, "What group is that?"

The answer: "Oh, that's the cancer support group."

"Why are they laughing?"

"Nobody knows."

It's even more amazing because most of the people in our group have medically incurable cancer. We cry together and pray together, and there's something very comfortable about being able to laugh together with people who are in the same boat as you.

Recently we laughed as a woman described how she had lost all her hair but was watching it slowly grow back. She proceeded to tell us in detail how many hairs she now had on each leg and under each

arm. I was concerned this was TMI (Too Much Information) and
wasn't sure how the first-timer next to her would react. But before
I could intervene, he piped up and asked, "Any on your chest?"

We laughed with the rectal cancer survivor—a middle-aged man
from a very conservative religious upbringing—who told us how
he'd put a mirror on his ceiling at the visiting nurse's suggestion to
help learn how to work with his colostomy bag when it was new. It
worked well and eventually he didn't need to use the mirror anymore. But he said he forgot to take the mirror down and got some
interesting looks when fellow church members came over to install
new carpet in his bedroom!

One of the most fun couples to attend the Cancer Prayer Support
Group was Doreen and Bill Hooker. In their native England, a hooker
is a small boat, not a woman of ill repute, so it took them awhile to
understand why Americans snickered every time they said their last
name.

But eventually they decided they might as well have some fun
with it too. This is how they always introduced themselves at our
support group.

"I'm Doreen."

"I'm Bill."

"We're the Happy Hookers!"

That intro always brought a smile to even the saddest new
patient at the meeting. (Doreen and Bill happened to be talking with
me when I got the call from a Tyndale editor telling me my first book
was going to be published. So I've always enjoyed telling people I got
the news "with a couple of Hookers in my office.")

Every time we laugh together at our group, it reminds us that we
are still alive . . . and that always is worth celebrating. If you don't
have a funny oncology nurse or a laughing support group nearby,

former major league pitcher Dave Dravecky's Outreach of Hope has a few suggestions to "strengthen your funny bone":

- Start your own comedy collection of jokes and cartoons. (Do an Internet search for "clean jokes" and you'll find some good laughs. Post them at your desk or on your fridge so you can remind yourself to laugh.)
- Get your groceries and get a chuckle by reading some of the tabloid headlines while standing in line. (I just read about aliens with anorexia, and manure as a miracle cure for arthritis!)
- Hang out at the greeting-card racks and enjoy reading funny cards (wash your hands first and don't eat an ice cream cone while you do this!). You can even live it up and buy a funny card to brighten a friend's day! (One day at work I received a card with an odd-looking old man on the front that said, "I bet I can still float your boat . . . even if I don't have both oars in the water!" It was from my wonderful husband to brighten my day.)
- Become a humorous people group by hanging out with funny people. (Either you're a funny friend or you need one!)
- Make the most of embarrassing moments. (Did I tell you about the time a pair of my underwear dropped out of the pant leg of my jeans onto the floor of a Christian bookstore while I was shopping there?—never mind . . .)[8]

◎ ◎ ◎

I believe God wants us to smile. In his book *The Purpose-Driven Life*, Rick Warren writes that our first purpose in life is to please God. Or as Warren puts it, "The smile of God is the goal of your life."[9]

Cancer can and often does take things away from us and from our families, but it needn't take away our goal in life—to please God—to make Him smile.

Nehemiah 8:10 says, "Do not grieve." Why don't we grieve? Because we don't have cancer? Because we are in remission? Because our loved one is cured? No, it doesn't say anything like that. It says, "Do not grieve, for the joy of the LORD is your strength" (NIV).

No matter what the status of our health or our loved one's health, we don't have to grieve; we can find strength as we enjoy the Lord.

Psalm 118:24 says, "This is the day the LORD has made. We will rejoice and be glad in it."

It's great to rejoice when you get good news as a cancer patient or as the loved one of a patient. But you don't have to wait until then to have joy!

The psalmist isn't waiting to rejoice until his cancer tumor marker comes down. He isn't waiting to rejoice until the PET scan looks good. He isn't waiting to rejoice until his loved one is pronounced in remission or cured. No, he's rejoicing now because it is a new day that the Lord has made and he's alive!

I'm so glad my friend Dorothy didn't think she had to wait for her hair to grow back to have joy. Instead she chose to make the most of life's embarrassing moments and find joy in them.

Just today our nurse Ruth added a new sign to her chemo room bulletin board. It's a quote from American philosopher William James, which says, "We don't laugh because we're happy. We're happy because we laugh."

Author Max Lucado explains in his book *When God Whispers Your Name* how we can find that kind of happiness.

It's quiet. It's early. My coffee is hot. The sky is still black. The world is still asleep. The day is coming.

In a few moments the day will arrive. It will roar down the track with the rising of the sun. The stillness of the dawn will be exchanged for the noise of the day. The calm of solitude will be replaced by the pounding pace of the human race. The refuge of the early morning will be invaded by decisions to be made and deadlines to be met.

For the next twelve hours I will be exposed to the day's demands. It is now that I must make a choice. Because of Calvary, I'm free to choose. And so I choose. . . .

I choose joy. . . .

I will invite my God to be the God of circumstance. I will refuse the temptation to be cynical . . . the tool of the lazy thinker. I will refuse to see people as anything less than human beings, created by God. I will refuse to see any problem as anything less than an opportunity to see God.[10]

No matter what you've gone through or what still lies ahead, will you choose joy? Will you choose to please God and bring a smile to His face? It is your choice. You can choose to keep (or get) a sense of humor even in cancer's shadow.

Did you hear about the ninety-two-year-old man who went to his doctor for a checkup? A few days later his doctor saw him on the street, smiling broadly with a gorgeous young woman on his arm.

The next time the elderly gentleman came in for a checkup, the doctor remarked, "You looked pretty happy when I saw you the other day. What's going on?"

"Just taking your advice," the gentleman replied. "'Get a hot mamma and be cheerful!'"

"I didn't say that," the doctor shot back. "I said, 'You got a heart murmur, be careful!'"

I have a blessing for you from the book of Numbers as you try to find the joy in cancer's shadow:

May the LORD bless you
and protect you.
May the LORD smile on you
and be gracious to you.
May the LORD show you his favor
and give you his peace.
(NUMBERS 6:24-26)

CHAPTER 6

Do I Positively Have to Stay Positive?

"You can beat this."

"Think positive."

"You can do it."

"Just stay positive."

I know people mean well when they say those things to cancer survivors, but I must admit they often rub me the wrong way.

Many caring people have uttered those kinds of "encouraging" phrases to me in the many years I've been living in cancer's shadow, but I always have had the feeling that the words have done more for the person saying them than they did for me.

In fact, rather than being comforting and encouraging, those phrases often created more distress in me. I'd think:

I'm worried the cancer is back, but I have to think positive so the cancer doesn't come back.

I'm discouraged thinking about all I've endured, but I have to think positive so I get healthier.

I'm sad because of the losses I've suffered with this disease, but I have to think positive so I better not cry.

And the real kicker:

If I don't get cured, it must somehow be my fault because I
didn't think positive enough!

Don't get me wrong: I am by nature an optimistic person who
usually gives others the benefit of the doubt and likes to find ways to
make the best of any situation. But I am also positively positive that
being positive *all* the time is *not* necessary for those living in cancer's
shadow.

In fact, trying to live life by being "up" all the time can create a
new problem: "the tyranny of positive thinking." That's the phrase
used by Dr. Jimmie Holland, chairman of the Department of Psychiatry and Behavioral Sciences at Memorial Sloan-Kettering Cancer Center. In her excellent book, *The Human Side of Cancer: Living with Hope,
Coping with Uncertainty*, she explains the phrase: "All this hype claiming that if you don't have a positive attitude and that if you get
depressed you are making your tumor grow faster invalidates people's
natural and understandable reactions to a threat to their lives. That's
what I mean by the tyranny of positive thinking."[11]

Dr. Holland further disputes the popular notion that stress alters
the immune system and therefore causes cancer. "The bottom line is
that the mind-body connection is clear—emotions affect hormones
and immune function—but that link between mind-body interac-
tions and cancer is far less clear and remains unproved," she writes.
"There is a vast difference between saying that stress temporarily
alters some function in the immune system and saying that stress,
therefore, causes cancer."[12]

The truth, Dr. Holland says, is that "stress, depression, and grief
do not increase the likelihood that cancer will develop or that it will
come back if you've been treated before."[13]

I was so relieved when I read Dr. Holland's book because it said all the things that I believe and have observed in my years as a patient advocate, but she has the initials and credentials after her name to back them up!

I am a believer in the mind-body connection between our thoughts and our health, and I fully believe that how we feel emotionally can affect how we feel physically. But I agree with Dr. Holland and totally reject the notion that somehow we can change our uncertain futures to *definite* cures by positive thinking.

Now if by some slim chance you are really the kind of person who likes to think positive all the time, copes with life by always thinking positive, and finds it impossible to think any other way, I certainly am not going to tell you to stop thinking positively. But please don't expect that everyone else needs to be just like you.

My friend Sally recently was diagnosed with colorectal cancer at the age of forty-eight. The diagnosis stunned her because of her relatively young age (more than 90 percent of colorectal cancer patients are over fifty) and otherwise excellent health. As she tried to absorb the shock of it all, her husband, Jerry—an always-positive person—kept assuring her that everything was going to be okay.

"My husband, the eternal optimist, is driving me crazy!" she told me, laughing, a few days before she had surgery.

Fortunately, the couple have a close, loving relationship and were able to communicate to one another their true feelings and needs. Jerry *needed* to think optimistically and Sally *needed* to get the facts and find out the possibilities she might be facing.

As Jerry had predicted, everything turned out well. The cancer was caught at an early stage and required no further treatment after surgery. But Sally also was right to cope in the way that fit her personality and allowed her to truly feel better about her uncertain future.

ⓔⓞ   ⓔⓞ   ⓔⓞ

You probably have your own special way of dealing with sadness and worry. When I polled my support group the other night concerning what they do when feeling down, I got an interesting array of answers.

Ruth, the twelve-year stage IV breast cancer survivor you met earlier in chapter 5, says she takes out her frustration on her computer: "I bang on the keys and say 'Why me? Why me?'" Of course, she doesn't get a response from her PC, but she says she feels better afterward and then starts to play an online computer word game and temporarily forgets her troubles.

Melina, diagnosed with stage IV colon cancer at age thirty-five, says she relies on her husband when she feels overwhelmed by her illness: "I talk to him and he always puts things in perspective and that really helps me."

During the past nearly six years that Deb's been fighting colon cancer, she also turns to her husband for comfort, and together they seek a change of scenery. "When I'm feeling sad, we pick a place and go away together."

Watching reruns of the TV show *M*A*S*H* is what lifts the spirits of Rod, diagnosed with tonsil cancer six years ago. "They always make me laugh," he explains.

When Diane was first diagnosed in her early sixties with breast cancer requiring chemo and radiation, she admits feeling pretty discouraged. "My [grown] kids were the ones who cheered me up by sending me funny cards, books to read, and videos to watch."

My friend Genie, whom you met in the first chapter, recently told our morning support group that she, too, has a plan when she feels sad. "I always pray, and if that doesn't work, I go shopping!" she says with a laugh.

No matter how you cope, I'd like to suggest that at least once in a while you go ahead and let yourself express the sadness you feel. Don't pretend it's not there or distract yourself or try and escape. Realize the value of tears and let them flow.

Sometimes what cancer survivors need most is not someone to explain things and make them better but just to "feel" along with them.

That's how I felt when my first pregnancy ended with a miscarriage in 1977, on Mother's Day of all days. As I sat in my hospital room afterward, many people stopped by and made comments such as: "You'll have more children." "You'll be okay." "Think positive." Even my husband tried to give me reassuring explanations concerning our devastating loss.

None of them made me feel any better. Later I told Ralph, "I didn't want you to say encouraging things to me. I wanted you to hold me and cry with me."

My goal as someone living in cancer's shadow is *not* always to be positive.

> *For everything there is a season,*
> *a time for every activity under heaven. . . .*
> *A time to cry and a time to laugh.*
> *A time to grieve and a time to dance.*
> ECCLESIASTES 3:1, 4

I believe God created us to feel many emotions and that life is best lived when we acknowledge those emotions and express them in a healthy manner. Moreover, I believe tears are really a gift from God

and that everybody—even positively positive people—benefits from
a good cry now and then.

I did some research on tears and I'd like to share a little "science
lesson" to prove my point.

If you ever tasted a tear trickling down your face, then you know
they are salty. But tears are much more than salty water. They're actually a complex combination of proteins, enzymes, lipids, metabolites,
and electrolytes. (I'm not sure what all those are either, but I know it's
more than just salt!)

We all have three different kinds of tears: normal tears that continuously keep our eyes lubricated; irritant tears that wash away for-
eign substances; and emotional tears we cry for reasons like sadness
and pain. Scientists who study tears can look at these tiny drops of
water and tell the difference between the first two types and the third
kind, because emotional tears have much more protein and less oil.

I'm probably more fascinated with tears than the average person
because my right eye "cries" all day long due to the scarring from my
chemotherapy. I've had two surgeries to try to correct the problem,
but doctors tell me my tear duct is scarred beyond repair and the
only recourse would be to build a fancy new plastic one. I haven't yet
decided to go this route, although my husband thought it sounded
fun when he heard that if I puffed on a cigarette I would be able to
blow smoke rings out of my eye with my artificial tear duct! A great
conversation starter at parties, I'm sure!

A few amazing facts about tears may help you appreciate why we
need to cry once in a while.

- Every tear has three layers, each of which has a different
  purpose. The inner layer coats the cornea; the middle layer,
  which is almost all water, provides moisture and oxygen to the

cornea; and the outer layer is an oily film that seals the tears on our eyes and slows evaporation.

- Two different glands create the layers. A small gland produces the inner and outer layers and a large gland under the upper eyelid produces the middle layer.
- Some tear researchers theorize that emotional tears carry hormones from the brain, which release calming endorphins and flush toxins out of the bloodstream. This helps our body return to a reduced-stress state.

Isn't it amazing how much intricacy went into the creation of tiny tears by our Creator! We definitely shouldn't ignore their beneficial value to us as we live in cancer's shadow.

That's why my friend Jutta, whom you met in chapter 4, enjoys a good cry every once in a while, even though she is an upbeat, positive kind of person.

"The only time I cry is as a cleansing for me," she says. "I'm not a crier. I'd rather laugh then cry."

Recently Jutta encountered a woman at church who apologized for the tears she was shedding in public. "I told her, 'The tears you're having right now are tears of cleansing. You don't have to be the strong one all the time,'" Jutta recalls.

I'm glad my dear friend Norma was willing to cry with me throughout my chemo ordeal. Norma, now cancer-free in her eighties, has survived two different breast cancers as well as uterine cancer diagnosed in 1978. Her first breast cancer diagnosis was just a few months before my colon cancer diagnosis, and she called me every month from her home in New York state to check on me.

"Wanna have a pity party?" she'd ask when she called.

I'd say sure, and for the next half hour we'd trade poor-me

complaints about the side effects of our treatments. Pretty soon we had done enough moaning and started laughing at ourselves for all the complaining we were doing. (The moral of the story: Pity parties are great once in a while; just keep them short and only invite friends who still like to laugh too!)

In fact, people like Norma and me who don't repress our tears may have better health, according to many "crying" researchers who think emotional tears may remove toxins from our bodies. Some even theorize that women tend to live longer than men because on average they cry twice as much as men!

ⓔⓔ   ⓔⓔ   ⓔⓔ

Do you know what the shortest verse in the Bible is? It's two little words in the Gospel of John, chapter 11, verse 35 (NIV).

Jesus wept.

Jesus was standing at the grave of His friend Lazarus surrounded by Lazarus's weeping sisters and other wailing friends and He, too, began to cry.

He could have said, "Everything's going to be okay!" After all, He knew He was about to raise Lazarus back to life. He could have said, "Don't worry, be happy!" After all, He knew that in moments their sorrow would be turned to joy.

But He didn't make any such positive-thinking comments. Instead . . . He wept.

I certainly don't pretend to know exactly why Jesus wept, but I believe He wanted those present to know He felt their sadness, too, and He wanted those of us reading this account one day to know He thinks it's positively all right to cry.

Many of us need to tell ourselves that truth: that weeping is not a sign of weakness or shame; that tears are indeed a gift from God to express our deepest feelings.

Men, especially, need some convincing to let the teardrops flow. Blaine, the esophageal cancer survivor you met in chapter 1, told me it was at least two months after his stunning diagnosis before he ever shed a tear.

Once while chatting with me at our office, he told me how well he was feeling despite having had more than three weeks of daily radiation by that point. "I really feel good and I'm eating good," he said. "But I finally cried the other day and that felt good too."

More than three years later, when Blaine talks about his cancer ordeal and return to health, his eyes still get misty. I've read statistics that show 45 percent of men say they never cry (compared to 6 percent of women), but I'm thankful for strong, courageous men like Blaine in my support group who aren't afraid to show emotion. After all, if the very Son of God could cry, I think they can too.

                       ◎◎   ◎◎   ◎◎

Can you imagine all the tears you've ever cried in your life? The ones when kids made fun of you on the playground and when you skinned your knee in the backyard. Don't forget the ones when your pet died and when your first love broke your heart. Think about the tears you shed when you had your first car accident and when you didn't have enough money to pay the bills.

Remember the tears when you heard it really was cancer and those you shed when someone who was treated with you lost his or her cancer battle? Don't forget those tears you let slip in the shower so you could wash them away before anyone could see.

But someone did see. The same One who created the complexity
of tears, saw—and remembers—every one of yours.

You keep track of all my sorrows.
You have collected all my tears in your bottle.
You have recorded each one in your book.
PSALM 56:8

I imagine some of us must have some pretty big bottles to store
all our tears! But why does God keep and record these little salty
drops?

I love the explanation given by author Joni Eareckson Tada, who
has been confined to a wheelchair since a 1967 diving accident left
her paralyzed from the neck down. She believes that one day God
will "make it up" to us for every sad time we've faced.

Every tear you've cried will be redeemed. God will give you
indescribable glory for your grief, not with a general wave of the
hand, but in a considered and specific way. Each tear has been
listed; each will be recompensed.

I've cried a few times over not having the use of my hands.
I think it's ironic that on the day in heaven when I finally get
back use of my hands so I can dry my own tears . . . I won't have
to: "He will wipe every tear from [our] eyes" (Revelation 21:4).[14]

I look forward to that day when God will wipe away the tears
from my watery right eye and show me how He has turned all my
sadness into greatness for His kingdom. But until that time, I am positively happy to know that I don't have to stay positive all the time.

CHAPTER 7

Isn't There a Faster Way to Wait?

"Why does it take so long to get back my blood work?"

"I have to hang on *the whole weekend* for the test results?"

"What do you mean the doctor can't see me until next week?"

"This waiting is killing me!"

Ever moaned any of these phrases? I sure have. I once made the mistake of scheduling a barium enema test on a Friday. I thought I would have ulcers by the time I *finally* got the results on Monday. I jumped every time the phone rang and worried every time it didn't.

The first few years after I finished chemo, I used to call and talk to the nurses prior to each of my follow-ups so I could get my tumor marker results *before* I went in for my appointment. I just couldn't stand to wait.

When I have to wait, my mind begins to wander, the bad little voice of fear starts to pipe up, and I usually begin to think the worst.

A few months after I finished my chemo, I had a CT scan for some terrible abdominal pain I was experiencing. The technician asked me to wait twice while she conferred with another medical person and came back and took more pictures. Each time she came back into the little room and looked at me, I became more and more convinced she looked sadder. I should have realized she probably

felt sorry for me in my pitiful little blue paper gown, but instead
I surmised I must be going to get terrible news.

Finally when she came back in for the third time—even though
I knew she wasn't allowed to say anything about the scan—I blurted
out: "Please tell me what's wrong. I know it must be really bad. Just
tell me; I can't stand this waiting anymore!"

She looked rather puzzled and reassured me that the only thing
wrong was that the pictures were not quite clear enough so she had
to take another set. I felt better for a moment and then decided she
probably was paid to say that to everyone.

I went home and waited for the call from my family physician.
When it came, my fear that a new tumor was obstructing my bowel
was quickly put to rest. Instead I was told that I needed to take a lax-
ative!

     ◎   ◎   ◎

I am convinced that those of us who are planners, who like to be prepared and who relish being in control, make the worst "wait-ers" on
the face of the earth. Waiting prevents us from planning, impedes us
from being fully prepared, and thwarts our attempt to be absolutely
in control of the present as well as the future.

My friends George and Carla know more about waiting in cancer's shadow than I do—or could ever hope to know. You learn a lot
about the subject of waiting when you are forced to wait more than
two years for a liver transplant and a chance to beat cancer.

Their pilgrimage of waiting actually began in May 2001 when a
mysterious abnormality showed up in George's blood when he tried to
donate a pint to the Red Cross. Finally in November the mystery was
solved after he was diagnosed with a rare bile-duct inflammation called

primary sclerosing cholangitis. (The bile duct is the tube that drains bile from the liver and gallbladder into the bowel.) Physicians told him that about 10 percent of the time this condition develops into cancer.

George was a young, healthy-looking forty-seven-year-old, so he hardly worried he would be in that small, unfortunate minority. Still he continued to seek medical opinions on whether anything should or could be done for the condition. In May 2002 a test at a nearby major medical center showed that George was in that small 10 percent group: The inflammation in his bile duct had become cancerous.

The news was devastating as every physician he saw "pretty much told me to go home and get ready to die because there's nothing to be done."

Every physician except one.

There was one specialist who told him, "The cancer is so small and you're so healthy, I just can't accept this." She arranged for him to be seen by another specialist at the world-famous Mayo Clinic that July.

George flew the three-hour trip from his home to the clinic where he was given an aggressive regimen of external beam radiation, radio-active isotopes, and chemotherapy to try to slow the cancer's progression. Doctors told him his only hope for a cure was to get a new liver from a transplant. Because he wasn't "too sick," they put his name near the bottom of the transplant list and sent him home to see an oncologist and continue getting chemotherapy to try to keep the disease in check.

Come back in three months, the Mayo doctors said.

   ⎈⎈ ⎈⎈ ⎈⎈

I saw George in the waiting room at our cancer center in the fall of 2002. We live in the same small town and our children attended school together, but I hadn't seen him for several years. I was surprised to find out he was waiting to see the oncologist who shares Marc's building.

He explained his diagnosis and told me that he really wanted to get the transplant soon while the cancer was small and while he felt healthy and had a good shot at a cure. But cancer patients are considered a poor risk for liver transplants, he said; besides, he wasn't sick enough.

We began to see one another regularly in the halls of our office or when he visited my support group as his work schedule permitted. I started praying he would get just sick enough to get a transplant, but not so sick as to die. Many other people at his church and throughout the community were praying for him. Both he and I felt confident that those prayers would be answered very soon.

When he was put on the United Network for Organ Sharing (UNOS) list in August 2002, he was given a very low priority score, which the Mayo Clinic appealed. It took seven months of long waiting, but in March 2003 he got the good news that his appeal was accepted—the only one of twenty-one appeals okayed by the powers-that-be that day. The new, higher score inched his name up on the list.

"I believe this is a definite answer to prayer," he told me one day at the office after sharing his good news.

"I still have to stay on chemo and pray the cancer doesn't go out of the liver because it will still take until fall to get a liver," he added.

But as the waiting game continued, George's health began to deteriorate. In June he developed blood clots in his liver and had to go on blood thinners. He thought doctors would put a stent (a small device implanted to keep a vessel open) in his liver because he was becoming increasingly jaundiced, but they decided they wanted him to get sicker so he could move up the transplant list. Mayo asked him to return in early August, and George hoped he would stay there to wait for his new liver.

But the Mayo doctors did some exploratory surgery, decided the cancer hadn't spread, and sent him back home. He was no longer physically able to keep up with his job as a welder and took a medical leave of absence.

Now there was plenty of time to do nothing but wait.

During the winter of 2003–2004, George and Carla continued to make the trek to the Mayo Clinic every three months while he remained on an oral chemotherapy monitored by his local oncologist. George fought infections five times and finally developed a blood infection in February 2004 that nearly took his life. His doctor prescribed stronger antibiotics and told him to stay on them until he got a transplant.

In March 2004, George and Carla headed back to the Mayo Clinic, where three stents were placed in his liver and gallbladder because of his severe jaundice. Another appeal was sent to UNOS, and again it was approved, giving him a higher priority status.

It appeared the wait would be over soon.

But it was another false hope. He had to get healthier because now he was too sick for a transplant.

In mid-May, after two more months of waiting—and three years after the blood abnormality first reared its ugly head—the call came that he was now at the top of the list for the next liver matching his blood type.

On their thirty-first wedding anniversary—May 19, 2004— George and Carla hopped on a plane to Rochester, Minnesota, and expected their wait to end in a matter of a few days. After all, five other candidates with George's type O blood had received new livers

in the past ten days. Surely God was ready to give a long-awaited
answer to their prayer.

But again the ordeal was not over quickly.

Instead the couple waited in the free lodging provided at the
"transplant house," making new friends with others in similar dire
situations. On May 30 George celebrated his fiftieth birthday and
waited to see if it would be his last.

On June 24 I got an urgent e-mail from Carla asking for prayers
for her husband. The bilirubin level (causing yellow jaundice) in his
blood had doubled, signaling that the stents in the liver were
blocked. If it continued to rise, doctors would have to replace the
stents to save his life. But that procedure also would mean he would
not be strong enough to survive a liver transplant and would lose his
coveted top spot on the list.

"We continue to lean on the Lord, for this is where our strength
comes from," Carla wrote in closing that e-mail.

I knew my voice was joining many others when I stopped everything I was doing that night and asked for God's divine intervention
in George's life.

At eleven the next morning the pager attached to George's belt
finally broke its long silence. "My wife and I were sitting and watching television when the pager went off and I said to my wife, 'There
it is.'"

A donor match had been found. After a few hours of last-
minute preparations, George headed into surgery at 9:30 p.m., and
by 4 a.m. on June 26, he had a new cancer-free liver. Three and a
half weeks later, much to his surprise and to his doctors' amazement, the liver was functioning so well that he was on his way home
to Pennsylvania.

As George reflects on his ordeal, he readily admits that many times he wondered why his prayers weren't being answered. "When we got the call to go to Mayo and then wound up waiting for five weeks [as] I started getting really sick again, I just really wondered what God had in store," he says.

The hardest moments were when he was the most physically ill. "Those were the most difficult times," he says. "When you're sick and in pain, you kind of question God and wonder, *What good am I doing when I'm feeling like this?*"

He admits he longed to be able to see ahead and know that all would be well, but instead "everything that has happened has been just in the nick of time."

"This has taught me a lot about patience," George adds. "I found myself out running ahead of God and this has taught me to let God lead the way and follow Him.

"People pray and they want it their way right now, but God sees miles ahead," he continues. "God hears our prayers and answers our prayers, but it's going to be in His way and not necessarily the way we think."

Three years is indeed a long time to wait in cancer's shadow, but for George the wait has been worth it all. "It's been an amazing journey," he says. "Our lives have been forever changed by what has happened. I guess I have to really thank God for all this—and I never thought I would say that!"

⊘⊘   ⊘⊘   ⊘⊘

Thank God for waiting? You've got to be kidding. I'm the kind of person who gets annoyed with slow dial-up connections on computers. I push elevator buttons repeatedly trying to make the doors close faster even though I've read that they automatically stay open for a predetermined number of seconds. I don't like to use my husband's cell phone because I have to press the numbers instead of speaking a name for automatic voice dialing. When I pray, I expect microwave answers, rather than having to wait for Crock-Pot responses.

Why should we ever be thankful for waiting? Because waiting reminds us that we aren't God, and that's an invaluable lesson for all of us. We, of course, would never declare, "I am God!" But every time we get impatient, annoyed, and frustrated with waiting, we demonstrate our need to be in charge. When we wait for others, it puts us at their mercy. They are controlling our schedules, our pace of life, and our agendas. Things are out of our hands.

Let's be honest: Most of us do not want to be at the mercy of someone or something else. But the Bible tells us that we are at God's mercy for every breath we take and that without His great mercy we can't ever see heaven.

For in him we live and move and exist.
ACTS 17:28

It is only by God's grace that you have been saved!
EPHESIANS 2:5

And every time we have to wait on God to answer our prayers, it reminds us that we are at His mercy. Waiting goes against our very nature but draws us closer to the Lord better than just about anything else.

Waiting is a common theme throughout the Bible—after God miraculously freed the Israelites from slavery in Egypt, they waited in the desert for forty years before He allowed them to enter the Promised Land. Jacob waited fourteen years to marry his beloved Rachel after he was tricked into virtual slave labor by his future father-in-law.

The disciples of Jesus waited three very long, agonizing days for Him to rise from the dead.

Often when we wait we become discouraged and are tempted to give up. The Israelites whined and moaned during most of their forty years of waiting. Jacob was furious when he discovered that his father-in-law had tricked him into marrying Rachel's older sister and he would have to work another seven years to marry Rachel. Following Jesus' crucifixion, the disciples gave up right away and were already back fishing before His resurrection.

When you're waiting, I have some advice for you. It's the same advice I tell myself when things are taking too long. Don't give up. Give in . . . to God.

Go ahead and put yourself at His mercy. That's where you already are anyway. You might as well admit it, because when you do, then you can start to experience the transforming power that waiting can have on our character.

Don't get confused. It's not that the waiting itself changes us—otherwise we all would be pretty wonderful people. After all, everybody has to wait sometimes! But it's how we *respond* to the waiting that can be transforming.

I love how author-pastor Rick Warren explains in *The Purpose-Driven Life* that godly characteristics—things like love, joy, peace, patience, kindness, goodness, gentleness, and self-control—are developed in our lives when we are put in situations in which we are tempted to respond exactly the *opposite* way.

Patience "is developed in circumstances in which we're forced to wait and are tempted to be angry or have a short fuse," Warren writes.[15]

I put this principle into practice one day recently while I braked for yet another red light on my hurried lunch-hour errand trip. I looked straight at the light, smiled, and said out loud to myself, "I am not waiting for a traffic signal. I am being conformed into the image of Jesus!"

The declaration made me laugh out loud—though hopefully not loud enough that any nearby motorist could hear me. But I'll tell you; it was a wonderfully freeing moment. I didn't squirm waiting for the light to change. I wasn't frustrated that I wasn't making good time. I just sat there and enjoyed the presence of God, which supernaturally settled over me.

Try it yourself.

> I am not waiting for test results. I am learning to depend more on God.
>
> I am not waiting for a doctor to call me back. I am learning to be patient as God is patient with me.
>
> I am not waiting in cancer's shadow. I am becoming more like Jesus.

Feel better about waiting? Just in case you need a little more encouragement about the positive benefits of waiting, I've compiled a list of my favorite verses on the subject. I hope you'll memorize a couple of them to encourage yourself the next time something or someone is taking too long!

> *Wait patiently for the LORD.*
> *Be brave and courageous.*
> *Yes, wait patiently for the LORD.*
> PSALM 27:14

> *I wait for you, O LORD;*
> *you will answer, O Lord my God.*
> PSALM 38:15 (NIV)

For since the world began,
 no ear has heard,
and no eye has seen a God like you,
 who works for those who wait for him!
ISAIAH 64:4

I wait for the LORD, my soul waits,
 and in his word I put my hope.
PSALM 130:5 (NIV)

But as for me, I watch in hope for the LORD,
 I wait for God my Savior;
 my God will hear me.
MICAH 7:7 (NIV)

We wait in hope for the LORD;
 he is our help and our shield.
In him our hearts rejoice,
 for we trust in his holy name.
May your unfailing love rest upon us, O LORD,
 even as we put our hope in you.
PSALM 33:20-22 (NIV)

There is no faster way to wait, but there is a *better* way.

CHAPTER 8

Can I Really Hear from God?

If you've gotten this far in the book (and not just skipped over to this chapter!), I think you can guess what my answer is going to be. Absolutely you can. Although I must warn you, it might not be as soon as you hoped and He might not speak in exactly the way you expect.

I continue to be amazed as I see God answer prayers in the lives of cancer patients and their loved ones. Sometimes it's not the answer we prayed for and other times it's exactly what was requested. But every time we hear from Him, it increases my faith that He really is listening and that He has the power to respond.

I'd like to tell you about two people who saw God answer prayers in their lives even though they both had doubted He really heard their anxious pleas. In fact, they had been sure they *wouldn't* hear from Him the way other people seemed to.

֍   ֍   ֍

It's easy to remember when I first met Maureen and her husband—it was the first anniversary of the September 11, 2001, terrorist attacks.

What a rotten day to have to start chemo, I thought as I talked with the couple in my office. Maureen was forced to reschedule this first treatment because the week before she had had to go to Nebraska where her mother took ill while visiting relatives.

This was our first face-to-face meeting, although we already had talked a couple of times on the phone concerning Maureen's worries about treatment for her newly diagnosed breast cancer. As I explained my job of offering emotional and spiritual support, I could see that she was especially anxious regarding all that lay ahead.

Maureen said she and her husband had gone to church early that morning to pray. I thought perhaps their visit was prompted by the day's special significance to our country, but she said they made the same visit most mornings before work.

Despite their faithfulness in these early morning prayers, Maureen admitted that she didn't feel she heard from God the way other people seemed to hear Him. Her husband concurred that the amazing things that happened to other people never seemed to happen to them.

"We just don't hear from God that way," he told me.

I didn't have any answer to their dilemma but asked if I might pray for them before Maureen's first treatment began in a few minutes.

They readily agreed, so we held hands in my office, and I prayed a prayer of blessing over them.

When I finished, Maureen had a shocked look on her face.

"I can't believe what you just prayed!" she said.

Oh dear, have I made some theological mistake? I wondered.

"What did I say?" I asked her, truthfully not remembering any special words I had just uttered.

"You prayed that I would have 'strength, courage, and peace,'" she said. "Those are the three things I have been praying for, in that exact order, every day since I was diagnosed with cancer."

"So much for not hearing from God!" I responded with a smile. "I don't think there's any doubt now that He heard your prayers!"

I was pretty excited at God's amazingly fast answer to this couple's desire to hear from Him, but He wasn't done with them yet that day.

Maureen went down the hall to get her IV hooked up, and I went into an exam room to talk with another patient named Dee. Dee started telling me that she wanted to loan my book to her next-door neighbor's daughter who was recently diagnosed with cancer. She added some details about how her neighbor had become ill while she was in Nebraska.

"Wait a minute," I said, stopping her story. "What's your neighbor's daughter's name?"

"Maureen," she replied.

I quickly dashed into the chemo room and asked Maureen if I had her permission to introduce her to her mother's neighbor and good friend. Within moments, introductions were made between the two women who had heard much about each other but had never met. The veteran patient, Dee, hugged the novice patient, Maureen, and assured her she had been praying for her.

"I am so excited," Maureen kept saying. "Things like this never happen to me!"

And that's how Maureen learned for sure that God really did hear her prayers and that His amazing power wasn't just something that happened to other people.

◎◎   ◎◎   ◎◎

My friend Eric's answer to prayer didn't come nearly as quickly, but it, too, came in the nick of time and was just as amazing.

When I saw Eric's name on the hospital census in June 2000, I just had to visit him. He had been diagnosed with colorectal cancer and was listed as age thirty-eight—just about the same age I was when diagnosed.

Eric hadn't been referred to our office yet, but I called his surgeon, who often refers patients to me, and offered to visit Eric at the hospital. The surgeon readily agreed and told me Eric had stage III disease, just as I had had.

I raced right over to the hospital while praying for my meeting with Eric, whom I was sure would be thrilled to meet another colorectal cancer survivor with a similar story. I never did pray *whether* or *when* I should visit him, only that God would bless our time together.

Big mistake.

I went into Eric's room and introduced myself to him and his wife, Kathy. Eric was in a lot of pain when I arrived, having just gotten up for his first postsurgerical walk. I quickly lowered my initial expectations that he would be "thrilled" to meet me. I decided "happy" to meet me would be fine.

Wrong again.

I introduced myself and said that I was a ten-year colorectal cancer survivor of stage III cancer diagnosed at the age of thirty-six. Before I got any further, Eric interrupted me. "Do you have a colostomy?" he said with a less-than-friendly look on his face.

"No," I replied sheepishly.

The resulting look in his eyes clearly conveyed: *You don't understand what I'm going through.* He shook his head and turned his gaze away. Never in my whole life have I wanted so badly to have a colostomy as at that moment.

"I have a lot of friends with colostomies," I told him in hopes that he somehow would feel I understood by association.

He didn't even respond.

This was a great idea coming in here. You really made this patient feel better. Is there a hole somewhere I can crawl into?

We made a little awkward small talk and I left the room as quickly as I had come in a few minutes before.

The next month, Eric was referred to our office for chemotherapy. I was on vacation that day so I just left a note for him. I remember thinking that he probably was relieved he didn't have to face me again.

The next time Eric came in, I was there and we chatted a little. It was obvious he was very angry about his diagnosis, and unlike most patients, he didn't even try to hide it.

Eric didn't fare really well during his treatments. He had a lot of side effects but continued working at least sixty hours a week at his job. He completed all his radiation treatments but ended up quitting chemo about a month or so before he was supposed to finish.

That next April when he went for a follow-up, the CT scan showed several large tumors in the liver and another tumor in the rectum. I could only imagine how angry Eric would be now.

I called his family doctor, who said Eric already had gone to Hershey Medical Center for a second opinion about surgery.

Eric turned out not to be a surgical candidate, so he decided to try some fairly new chemo that had been approved for recurrent colon cancer. As we chatted during his first return visit in May 2001, he mentioned that a lot of people had put his name on their church's prayer chain, where each member telephones the next to ask for prayer for an individual.

"Yeah, I'm on a lot of prayer chains, but everyone is getting a busy signal," Eric told me.

Because I could see he was so discouraged, I decided to send him a little note sharing my thoughts about the struggles of getting "bad news" and encouraging him to put his hope not just in a physical cure, but in God's unchangeable love for him. I mailed it to him so that in case it made him madder, I wouldn't be there to see it!

The next time Eric came in for a visit I certainly had no plans to bring up the contents of my note, but he did.

"I read all the stuff you sent me," he said. "I have my own philosophy."

"Oh, what's that?" I said, half afraid to hear his answer.

"I don't want to make Jesus my number one priority because if I do He'll take me Home," Eric explained. "My family is my number one priority and Jesus will just have to stay number two. I figure that as long as He's second best, He'll let me live because He'll want to give me time to make Him first."

I had never heard this line of reasoning before, but then Eric wasn't one who did things by the book. I didn't argue with him and in fact felt very delighted that Jesus was number two, as I didn't think He would have rated that high with Eric!

I didn't tell Eric, but I secretly prayed that he would love God more than anything else and trust Him to care for his family too. A couple of months later I began to see how that prayer was being answered. As we sat talking in the chemo room during his treatment, Eric told me that he couldn't sleep one night that week so he "talked to God."

"We talked for about twenty minutes," he said. "I just told Him everything I was thinking and feeling, and I told Him I couldn't handle this all by myself and I really needed Him and His strength. I told Him I still don't want to go to heaven yet, but I really want His help."

It was fourteen months since Eric had been diagnosed with cancer, and that was the first time I heard this incredibly self-sufficient man admit he needed God. I knew that prayer was a defining moment in his cancer journey as he tried to find the light in cancer's shadow.

He continued his explanation. "I'm not going off the deep end or anything."

"What do you mean by that?" I asked.

"I'm not going to walk around saying 'Praise the Lord' all the time," he quickly explained.

I laughed as I assured him that that had never been my goal for him and that I only wanted him to experience the joy of knowing God and walking with Him each day.

Eric added that the day after that night of prayer he felt really good physically and even ate a foot-long sandwich from his favorite sub shop—something he hadn't been able to do for months.

"I know that was from God," he said.

When I talked with Marc later that day, he commented that Eric seemed a lot happier and nicer. The two of them had never really hit it off, but from that day forward their relationship changed and they got along quite well.

In March 2002 Eric got more bad news in his battle with widespread cancer. As he, his wife, Kathy, and I sat talking in the exam room, it was obvious this latest blow really upset both of them.

"Could I pray with you?" I gingerly asked, still never sure how Eric might react.

"Pray all you want—He doesn't hear me," came Eric's disheartened reply.

The three of us joined hands and I prayed that this dear young couple could feel God's love for them in spite of their circumstances. When I finished, Eric said through choke-filled tears, "He doesn't hear me. He doesn't hear me."

The couple talked with Marc about another possible chemo combination and some new pain medication. As they were leaving, Eric stopped me in the waiting room, thanked me profusely for the prayer, and hugged me two or three times.

"I don't think God remembers me," he said with tears running down his face.

I promised Eric that not only did God remember him, but He also promised He never would forget him (see Isaiah 49:14-16).

"Well, I need a sign from God that He remembers me and hears my prayers," Eric flatly announced.

"That will be my prayer for you, Eric, that you get a sign," I said.

I had no idea what kind of sign would convince Eric of God's unfailing love for him, but I followed up that conversation with an e-mail to Eric and Kathy a few days later that said, "I'm especially praying that you can sense the Lord's presence and peace in your hearts and that Eric will get 'a sign' that will assure him God really does love him and hears his cries!"

A couple of months later Eric was on hospice and failing quickly. I began visiting him at home to chat and pray. On one visit I asked him if he still was angry with God and he answered no. But as tears filled his eyes, he said, "Well, maybe I am just a little."

Then he added, "I guess God is doing His best for me."

I told Eric that no matter what does or doesn't happen to any of us in this life, God already *has* done His best for all of us. He did that when He sent His one and only Son to walk this earth as a sinless person and then die on the cross to pay for the sins of every person.

"When we put our faith and trust in Jesus, we always get God's best: eternal life," I concluded.

Kathy joined us in the bedroom shortly and we all prayed together.

"I don't like a lot of women, but I'm making an exception for you," Eric told me with a big grin.

With that huge endorsement, I felt confident continuing to visit, pray, and read the Psalms weekly with Eric.

"I'm going to get a copy of your book, right?" he asked me during one visit in early May. *When God & Cancer Meet* was due to be published July 1, and Eric was very excited to read it because I had shared a couple of the chapters with him as I was writing them. He especially enjoyed Lynn and Jane's story on God's faithfulness in the midst of life's unfairness.

"I will get one here as soon as it's out," I responded, knowing realistically there was no way Eric would still be alive in two months. To complicate things further, I had even been warned by my publisher not to be disappointed if the book came out later than originally scheduled.

"Promise me you'll give me a book," he insisted.

"I promise to get a book to your house as soon as it's published," I hedged again.

Two weeks later I went to visit Eric but he didn't wake to see me. Kathy said he was sleeping almost constantly and the hospice nurses felt death was imminent.

I wrote in my patient progress notes at work on May 23: "I don't think I'll get to see Eric again, but that is okay as we have said our good-byes."

Five days later I got an e-mail from my publisher saying that my book had been printed—six weeks early. I called my publicist in Chicago with the exciting news. She, however, was not thrilled because the necessary publicity was not in place. She told me to call Tyndale and ask them to hold the book until the original release date, which I quickly did.

Great, my book is published but no one can even see it yet! What's going on here, Lord?

I woke very early the next morning (something I rarely ever do) and God immediately spoke to my heart: *Get a book to Eric.*

Being a first-time author, I had no clue as to how things like this work and whether I could get a copy before the release date. But I called the Tyndale office and said that I had a dying friend who wanted to see the book. I explained that he was semicomatose, and even if they sent the book overnight I didn't know if he still would be alive when it arrived. I didn't think there was any chance he would be alert enough to actually see the book, but I wanted to try.

"The last overnight drop leaves our office in thirty minutes," the Tyndale staff person told me. "I think I can just make it."

"One quick question," I said. "Do you know why my book came out so early?"

She said that it was indeed strange for a book to come out so early and she had no idea how or why it had happened. I called Kathy and told her to tell Eric that the first copy of my book would be at their home tomorrow. I prayed he would live long enough to at least hold the book in his hands because it seemed to mean so much to him.

Kathy called me the next day. I could tell in her voice that she was choking back tears.

"Eric got the book," she said. "He was awake and really good today. We already read the first three chapters to him. His mom was crying so hard she could hardly see the words on the pages when she read it to him—thank you so much!

"Eric says he wants you to come over and sign the book," Kathy added.

I was so glad to hear the old Eric was back telling me what to do!

I went to his house to sign my book. It was an awesome moment. I signed it in part: "The very first copy of my very first book—WOW!"

Then I swallowed hard and told Eric: "I think God published this book early as a sign to show you how much He loves you and that He heard your prayers."

With tears in his eyes, Eric replied, "That is what I think too."

The last time I visited Eric was June 10. He was very weak and his voice was just a whisper, but his mind was clear and coherent despite a steady stream of narcotics from his morphine pump.

I promised him that if I ever wrote another book, I would write about him and God's special sign for him. He nodded okay. We sat for a few moments in silence as I held his hand and savored thinking about all the Lord had done in his life.

Eric broke the silence. "Now, get out of here," he whispered with a smile.

And so our relationship ended just as it had begun, with Eric chasing me out of his room. He passed away the next day, still three weeks shy of the book's release date.

❧   ❧   ❧

I hope that Eric's story encourages you that God does indeed hear prayers. He hears *your* prayers—prayers that you want to live; prayers that you want to see your children grow up or your grand-children married or maybe even hold a great-grandchild. He hears when you tell Him that you want to think about life without cancer or maybe living with cancer instead of dying from it.

He hears your prayers even if, like Maureen, you can't imagine He will give you an amazing answer. He hears your prayers even if you're angry or doubting or confused as my friend Eric was and as I have been, too, at times through the many years that I have lived in cancer's shadow.

I must confess that after I finished treatment I prayed, "Lord, I want to live and I want to forget about cancer. I just want to put it behind me and not think about it."

I think those of us living in the twenty-first century expect instantaneous everything. We press a computer key and we instantly receive e-mails from around the world. We push a TV remote button and instantly we are entertained. We touch a microwave pad and instantly we have food cooking. We complain if computers are too slow and feel irritated if someone doesn't have call-waiting and we get a busy signal. Likewise, I wanted to pray this prayer *one time* and have God answer it instantaneously so I didn't have to pray it again.

But even though we pray and God *instantly* hears us, He may or may not instantly answer us. Prayer can be hard work as we continually bring our requests before our Maker.

> *O LORD, hear me as I pray;*
> > *pay attention to my groaning.*
> *Listen to my cry for help, my King and my God,*
> > *for I pray to no one but you.*
> *Listen to my voice in the morning, LORD.*
> > *Each morning I bring my requests to you and wait*
> > > *expectantly.*
>
> PSALM 5:1-3

Notice that part about "each morning"? Taking our requests to God is something we need to do continually. I think every morning is a really good idea. Often I begin praying in the morning even before my feet hit the floor and my eyes are fully opened. I pray thanking God for another day and His blessings to me. And I pray asking Him for what my loved ones and I will need to face the day.

I pray and I wait expectantly—expecting that God will answer in His own time and His own way. He has answered some of my prayers exactly as I wanted: I am still alive, and in the spring of 2004, I watched my youngest daughter lead the student body procession for her university's graduation.

But some of my prayers He answered exactly the opposite of what I wanted: I haven't put cancer behind me and forgotten about it. In fact, it is pretty much the focus of every day of my life. And the really amazing part is that I'm *glad* He didn't answer my prayers the way I wanted, because I would have missed seeing Him work in some unforgettable ways. I hope you are glad He didn't either.

If He had . . . you wouldn't be reading this book, would you?

CHAPTER 9

Will Life Ever Be Normal Again?

This question is a very easy one to answer. The answers are yes, no, and I hope not.

Don't you feel better now?

Seriously, those really are the answers because the question is such a multifaceted one.

If you are asking, *Can I ever feel good physically like I did before I was treated for cancer?* the answer is an unequivocal yes.

On Mondays, a different patient walks through the door of our oncology office every fifteen minutes for a recheck appointment. Some finished treatment a few months ago; others were treated many years ago. Most of them are feeling very well and are back to normal workdays or retirement pleasures. I really like Mondays because they always remind me that there is life after cancer for many, many people.

One such "recheck" patient I always enjoy seeing is another man named Eric—this one, our very own version of Lance Armstrong. Eric was diagnosed with testicular cancer in 1987 at the age of thirty-one. Like Lance, Eric had stage IV cancer, which had spread to his liver, lung, and groin in 1988. Then in 1995 a solitary mass showed up in his brain. It was removed in surgery and turned out to be a benign cyst.

Now seventeen years after his diagnosis, Eric remains cancer-free and is enjoying life with his wife and three grown children. Despite such a devastating diagnosis at such an early age, Eric's physical health and strength have been restored and life for him in that sense is normal again.

I always was an active person before my cancer diagnosis, working out at the local YMCA three days a week for about ninety minutes per day. But I was so weak and sick during my chemo that I had to put my membership on hold for many months. Even when I first finished chemo I couldn't keep up with my aerobics class. Eventually I returned to my usual exercise routine and have continued to exercise almost daily ever since.

When patients finish treatment, they often ask me, "How long will it take to feel good again?" That is a more difficult question to answer because there are so many variables. Suffice it to say that you might begin to feel very good within a few weeks after treatment, but don't be discouraged if it takes much longer.

I finished my treatment in early February 1991, and in late April, Ralph and I went away for a "Celebrate Completing Chemo" weekend at a Victorian bed-and-breakfast in Cape May, New Jersey, with our friends George and Gigi. I remember thinking that I was feeling really great at the time and was back to normal. But Gigi remembers me looking somewhat pale and still not up to my usual speed.

She was right. I had felt crummy and become used to a "new normal" for so long that I had forgotten what "old normal" felt like. By August, six months after finishing chemo, I really did feel great and was finally back to my precancer normal.

ᏯᏰ ᏯᏰ ᏯᏰ

Now if you're wondering whether your life ever will be back to normal in the sense that you will be exactly the same person you were before cancer, the answer is no. Facing a life-threatening illness changes us. As the saying goes, it might make us better or it might make us bitter, but it changes us.

> You and your loved ones have faced a tremendous challenge.
> You have come face-to-face with your own mortality.
> You have endured difficulties you probably never thought you
>   could.
> You have learned to distinguish between the important stuff
>   and unimportant stuff.
> You know better than most that life is indeed a gift not to be
>   wasted.

When you've come through an experience like that, I hope you don't go back to life exactly as it was before.

Just after being diagnosed with cancer, I was in the hospital for my colon surgery over the Fourth of July holiday, and my roommate, who had had back surgery, was complaining about the weather. The forecasters were calling for rain and it was going to ruin her family's picnic plans. She and her family went on and on about how terrible this was and how they were so tired of all this rain.

I wanted to shout, "I'm fighting for my life and you're complaining about a picnic getting rained out?"

Thankfully, I kept quiet, but I did pray, *Please, God, may I never again grumble about the weather.*

I'm pretty sure I have kept that promise, although as time goes by it gets tempting to go back to "normal" and allow my moods to be decided by the temperature outside.

Not only did I stop complaining about certain things, having cancer really tightened my bonds with family and friends too. I still have all the hundreds of encouraging cards people sent me in those early dark days after my diagnosis. Many of them wrote notes of appreciation, thanking me for things I'd done that I never realized were special to them. I felt as if I were getting to hear my own eulogy without having to die first! It was wonderful.

Since that time I have made a point of trying to let people know how much and why I appreciate them. I wrote long letters to my parents thanking them for all their wonderful gifts to me through the years, and I often try to convey to my three daughters that they are life's biggest blessings to me.

Every time I see one of my daughters reach another milestone—a graduation, a new job, a first apartment, a really special boyfriend—it makes me cry because I am so thankful to be alive to see it. If I had not had cancer when my daughters were so young—which made me wonder whether I'd get to see them grow up—I would not appreciate these events in the same way. I believe we have an extra closeness today because they know they could have lost their mother and they, too, are grateful for the "extra" time we've had together.

                 ◎   ◎   ◎

My friends Jason and Jenn know a lot about being grateful for extra time, and they've also questioned whether life will ever return to normal again. Their story could fill a book, and hopefully Jenn, a newspaper reporter, will write one someday. But in the meantime, I'd like to let you see what cancer has taught them about normalcy and why they hope they nev1er go back to their old normal life.

One day in March 2001, Jason and Jenn were on their way home from having their income taxes done. They were both upset that, unlike the previous year when they got a refund, this year they owed money to the government.

As Jason slid his six-foot frame into the passenger seat of Jenn's small car, he felt a painful lump in his testicle. It was just one week before the five-year anniversary of completing treatment for the stage IV testicular cancer he had been diagnosed with just days before his twentieth birthday.

In a split second, taxes and money didn't seem at all important anymore.

Jenn and Jason were friends when he was first diagnosed with cancer in 1996 and began dating the next year after treatments were finished. At the time, they both felt confident he was cured and say they really never gave a second thought to a recurrence. (So much for the *guaranteed* power of positive thinking!)

When the new lump surfaced, they headed straight to Hershey Medical Center, where Jason had been treated with chemo and radiation while he was a sophomore at Penn State studying to become an elementary school teacher.

This time, the Hershey surgeons decided his testicle had to be removed. The couple remained optimistic, since Jason already had "banked" some sperm back in 1995 just in case he later encountered fertility problems and needed it to create a family.

But their optimism was short-lived as the cancer quickly spread to Jason's back and abdomen. He endured more chemo and radiation, and the disease went into remission again.

By the fall of 2002, Jason still was teaching fourth grade but was in constant pain, the source of which doctors were unable to diagnose. Finally in mid-December he fell at home and discovered he couldn't move his legs.

Jenn knew she wanted her husband's familiar physicians at Hershey Medical to treat this latest emergency, so she managed to drag him up onto a desk chair with wheels. She then got him into the car for the one-hour drive.

There doctors made a grim discovery: two tumors compressing the spine had paralyzed Jason from the waist down. A team of high-powered specialists came together and decided on more chemo and radiation.

About three weeks later, I met Jason for the first time when I spoke at his church in a neighboring community. He had read my first book and wanted to hear me speak that Sunday. He still was taking treatments and in rehab to try to learn to walk again.

That morning he left his wheelchair at home and dragged his legs using a metal walker. Watching him struggle to walk over to me was heartbreaking. He said he was "honored" to meet me, but I knew I was the one who was honored to meet someone who had suffered so much with such grace and perseverance.

Our friendship continued through e-mails, chats in my office, and visits to my support group. I could see that against all odds his life again was becoming more normal. By June 2003 he finished his treatments and rehab and miraculously was walking on his own again. Before another year went by, he played flag football with kids at church, attempted a little rock climbing and roller skating, and even joined an over-thirty men's basketball league. ("I can pass for thirty," the twenty-eight-year-old says with a grin, adding that his youth is not an unfair advantage because "my vertical leap is about one inch.")

As I write this, Jason has had almost two years without treatments and nearly two-and-a-half years without any recurrences. He continues to teach and even has gone back to school himself to finish his master's degree. He leads a Bible study at church for teenage boys, while Jenn continues to be a youth-group adviser.

Life almost seems normal again. "We're approaching the sense of normalcy and that makes me nervous," Jason says. Part of the nervousness stems from not wanting to get too settled and then have a jolting reality of another recurrence. (Doctors have told the young couple they no longer are trying to cure the cancer, but instead stay one step ahead of it.)

The rest of the nervousness is because Jason remembers how life was before cancer—before they treasured every day and each other as they do now.

"We would argue about stupid stuff. We still have little arguments, but we quickly resolve them now and we appreciate the little things in life. We're not normal—in a good way," he explains.

Jason also doesn't want to go back to living life the way he was. Despite having come to a personal faith in Jesus at the age of seventeen and being active in Christian groups on the Penn State campus, Jason's faith had grown cold near the end of college.

"Religion got to be a chore for me," he explains, "and I decided to forget the 'Christian thing' for a while."

He stopped reading his Bible, made excuses to skip church, and "just felt like I didn't need God," he recalls. When he did attend worship he was "pooh-poohing the pastor and ridiculing the music."

"I would come home and play my heavy-metal music to try and get the church stuff out of my head," he recalls. Then came the first recurrence, which was a spiritual wake-up call for Jason as it is for so many others I've met. "I realized I really did need God," Jason says.

He made a decision to quit playing at his faith and truly love God with his whole heart. That decision produced practical changes in their lifestyle.

"Normal for me [before cancer] would have been having a wife, having kids, sitting around in the evening socializing and watching TV," he says.

"Normal for me now is seeking purpose for my life and living it out," explains Jason who just finished "40 Days of Purpose" with his church, which is studying *The Purpose-Driven Life.*

Jason also is glad he's not "normal" in the way he views life and death. "For most people, it's normal to fear death; avoid it at all costs and do all you can to survive, because death is an awful thing," he says. "Normal is to think you're not going to die and everybody else is.

"I'm pretty sure I'm going to die before the other people I know," he continues, "but I don't fear death. Death isn't an awful thing if you love God and you're going to heaven."

And that is why when Jason thinks of returning to a "normal life" as it was before cancer, he says, "I hope not."

༺ༀ༅   ༺ༀ༅   ༺ༀ༅

How has your cancer journey changed your normal life?

I pray that everything cancer took away from you physically will be restored. Other than my weepy right eye and a few more trips to the bathroom each day, my health has been completely restored to what it was.

> *You have allowed me to suffer much hardship,*
> *but you will restore me to life again*
> *and lift me up from the depths of the earth.*
> *You will restore me to even greater honor*
> *and comfort me once again.*
> PSALM 71:20-21

> *Then I will make up to you for the years*
> *that the swarming locust has eaten,*
> *the creeping locust, the stripping locust and the gnawing locust.*
> JOEL 2:25 (NASB)

I also pray that all the new truths cancer has revealed will endure and that, in that way, your life will not go back to normal. I hope that certain feelings remain.

> The feeling that living to an old age is not guaranteed.
> The feeling that we ultimately are not in control.
> The feeling that the eternal things are far more important than the temporal ones.
> The feeling that we're blessed to be alive.

I especially pray that you would allow your journey with cancer to change you spiritually. I wasn't like Jason when I was diagnosed with cancer. I wasn't far away from God, rebelling against Him or living as my own god. In fact, just the opposite. I had a close, personal relationship with God, tried to serve Him each day, and wanted to live as if Jesus was both the Forgiver of my sins and the Leader of my life.

Still, I am changed spiritually because of my cancer journey.

Suffering does that to us if we allow it. I am a better person for having suffered. I have more compassion, more empathy, more patience, and more mercy.

> *Dear brothers and sisters, whenever trouble comes your way, let it be an opportunity for joy. For when your faith is tested, your endurance has a chance to grow. So let it grow, for when your endurance is fully developed, you will be strong in character and ready for anything.*
> JAMES 1:2-4 (NLT-1)

We also exult in our tribulations, knowing that tribulation brings
about perseverance; and perseverance, proven character; and
proven character, hope; and hope does not disappoint, because the
love of God has been poured out within our hearts through the
Holy Spirit who was given to us.
ROMANS 5:3-5 (NASB)

The bottom line is that suffering can make us less normal and
more like Jesus.

Perhaps your life is somewhat like Jason's was. You believe there
is a God and you even pray once in a while but that's about the extent
of your faith. God wants to do so much more in your life. Jesus said,
"I came that they may have life, and have it abundantly" (John 10:10,
NASB). He didn't come to take away the fun of life but to give it real joy.

I have loved you even as the Father has loved me. Remain in my
love. When you obey my commandments, you remain in my love,
just as I obey my Father's commandments and remain in his love.
I have told you these things so that you will be filled with my joy.
Yes, your joy will overflow!
JOHN 15:9-11

Just as a good parent knows what's best for his or her child, our
heavenly Father knows what is best for us and what will really make
us feel fulfilled. He and only He can fill the longing that each of us
has for something more than this life has to offer.

If you haven't already, I pray you will let God fill the hole in your
heart and make you *whole* by establishing a relationship with Him
through His Son, Jesus the Messiah. Everything else you put in that
hole—work, sports, music, people, food, drugs, alcohol—to try to fill
it up will only make it bigger.

I agree with the seventeenth-century French mathematician Blaise Pascal who said, "There is a God-shaped vacuum in the heart of every man which cannot be filled by any created thing."

You were created to know God, to love God, and to live for God. If that's not your normal life, then my fervent prayer is that life after cancer will not be normal for you ever again!

Search me, O God, and know my heart;
  test me and know my anxious thoughts.
Point out anything in me that offends you,
  and lead me along the path of everlasting life.
PSALM 139:23-24

CHAPTER 10

Will It Come Back?

Are you or your loved one the ideal patient?

I'm not asking whether you do everything the doctors tell you to do. I'm not referring to whether your disease is easily treatable. And I'm not talking about whether you have the right personality.

What I do mean is this: Do you have just the right blend of realism and faith as you live wondering when and if the cancer will come back? My boss calls someone with that perfect blend "the ideal patient," and I agree.

The first time I ever heard Marc use that term and its definition was with our patient Beth and her husband, Josh. By the time I met this wonderful couple, they already had traveled a difficult road and yet managed to hang on to faith in spite of life's unfairness.

If you haven't yet achieved "ideal" status, I pray Beth's story will boost you to that coveted spot, and if you're already there, I pray it reminds you that it's definitely the best place to be.

Beth was diagnosed with breast cancer in 1988 at the age of twenty-nine, when her firstborn was only one year old. She went through surgery, chemotherapy, and radiation, and was in remission until 1994 when the disease spread to her bones. I didn't meet her until 1999 after she and her husband moved to our area to start a new business and she became a patient of Marc's.

They now had three teenage daughters, and Beth told me that her spiritual faith was her number one priority in life. We easily became friends and usually prayed together each month when she came in for her bone treatment. I especially enjoyed our times together because after I prayed for her and her family, she always prayed for me and mine.

Beth had a strong desire to share her faith with her neighbors and an even stronger belief that God would heal her. She came from a faith tradition that believes firmly in the power of prayer, and she never seemed to doubt that He would answer her with a miracle.

Sometimes I meet patients who take Beth's faith one step further and *insist* they will be healed. I never argue with patients who are absolutely positive they are going to get better. There's no point because either they will be proven correct or they won't, and it doesn't really matter what I think.

So Beth and I continued to pray for her complete healing, absolutely believing God *could* do it and feverishly praying that He *would*.

But despite both our prayers and many, many more on her behalf, Beth kept getting bad news. Her breast tumor markers were up, the bone scan was worse, and finally the cancer spread to her lungs and then to her liver.

She was getting tired of treatments and was discouraged that she had not been healed. She knew her Bible well and often read and quoted verses that talked about God as a healing God and described His mighty power. But still the symptoms remained.

We chatted in the office Christmas Eve day in 2001. "I intellectually know the truth but it's hard to feel it emotionally," she told me through her tears. Beth hardly ever cried, so I knew she was really low.

"Why doesn't God heal me?" she asked.

That is one of the most difficult questions a person, especially a believer, can ask. It is very hard to reconcile the truth of a loving, all-powerful God who doesn't seem to be responding in a way we know He can.

"I, too, believe God is always a healing God," I told her, "and I absolutely believe He *will* heal you . . . but the timing might not be as you have prayed."

Then I lent her my favorite book on the subject, *When God Doesn't Heal Now* by Larry Keefauver. In it he explains that God always heals believers but He does so in His own sovereign timing.

"We cannot schedule this 'right time' for healing based on our opinions or rationale," Keefauver says.[16]

Most believers tend to take one extreme position or the other—either that God doesn't do miraculous healings today or that God always heals the sick if they have enough faith. I believe Keefauver's position is a much more biblical one.

When Beth brought back the book a few weeks later she, too, agreed. I could tell her heart was more at peace concerning her seemingly unanswered prayer. Her faith in God was just as strong as ever and her prayers for healing just as fervent as ever, but she had been reminded of the most important part: not my will, but Yours be done.

"We still stand on the promises and put our faith in His trustworthiness but also recognize His right to do whatever pleases Him with our lives," she wrote to me in a note shortly after our "healing" conversation.

"After all," she added, "we gave Him that right years ago" referring to when she and Josh had put their faith in God.

A few weeks later, I sat in with the couple as they met with Marc. They had just gotten more bad news on Beth's latest CT scan, and Marc was suggesting yet another kind of chemo to try to slow the tumors' progress. Josh posed the question that was on my mind but

I never would have asked. "Best-case scenario, Doc. If this chemo works well, will Beth be here in a year?"

Marc assured him that there was still reason to be optimistic that his wife's cancer could continue to be a chronic condition, rather than an imminent life-threatening one, and that another remission could happen. The three of us nonphysicians breathed a sigh of relief and then Marc made the unusual pronouncement that Beth was the "ideal" patient.

"You are realistic and realize that your situation is very serious, but yet you have faith that God can still do the miraculous," he said. "I call that the ideal patient."

Then we joined hands as the couple prayed, "It's all about Your will, Lord, not ours."

I loved Marc's assessment of Beth. According to some people's way of thinking, her and her husband's faith were diminished because they did not believe *absolutely* that Beth would be healed here on earth.

But I believe that their faith actually was increased as they refused to demand their own way and surrendered even more to God's way. I personally think it takes even more faith to continue to trust God, stand on His promises, and cling to hope when you aren't healed.

I never had the false assumption that if I had enough faith I would be healed. I knew that hundreds of people had prayed for my husband's first wife, Pat, when she was diagnosed with Lou Gehrig's disease while she and Ralph were still newlyweds. Many had prayed over her, including the great healing evangelist Kathryn Kuhlman. Other believers had anointed her with oil, fasted for and prayed for her while "speaking in tongues," but Pat still died. I never met her, but I know from those who knew her that she was a beautiful woman who loved the Lord with all her heart.

It was obvious to me that if all *that* didn't work to heal her, there was nothing else I could do to guarantee healing for myself. I look at that now as Pat's special gift to me because it helped me become the "ideal patient" with the right balance of realism and faith. I learned to do what was suggested by the title of the book by Pastor Adrian Rogers: *Believe in Miracles but Trust in Jesus.*

A lot of people want it to be the other way around as they look to miracles to prove their faith in God.

I know of another strong Christian woman who was diagnosed with incurable cancer in her thirties. She refused to believe that God wasn't going to miraculously heal her.

Her family also clung tenaciously to their unwavering faith. They even went so far as to screen all her mail to make sure there was no reference from anyone to anything but complete faith in a miraculous healing.

"I have confessed my healing," she told me during a phone conversation. "I have read many healing books. . . . I have prayed, prayed, prayed, confessed, and cried. Many others have wept and prayed for me. Still my symptoms remain and I cannot see any signs of my healing."

She passed away shortly after that. I always wondered how her family handled her death and whether they ever were prepared for it.

   ◎◎   ◎◎   ◎◎

It is *not* a lack of faith to accept whatever God's will is for us. If God's light is truly brighter than cancer's shadow, then we can trust His will for us. I believe it is a true sign of faith to trust Him no matter what happens in this lifetime.

Sometimes well-meaning friends can discourage cancer patients and their families when they try to spur them on to an absolute belief in an imminent physical healing.

Beth once told me that some of her good Christian friends stopped by the house one day to pray for her.

"They weren't too accepting of the fact that I'm not getting healed," she said. "They prayed over me really loudly and intensely, but that only made me feel worse."

Another patient I'll call Laura had a similar experience. She attended a church that had "healing classes," and one of the pastors visited her often when she was receiving hospice care.

Laura says she dreaded seeing him coming because she always felt worse after he prayed for her.

"I think he's really disappointed in me that I'm not getting healed," she says. "I guess he feels like I'm making him look bad, and he just doesn't know what to do with me."

If you have been insisting that God has to keep your cancer from coming back or is going to heal it if it already has returned, I pray you will step back for just a moment and remember who is the Creator and who is the created.

What sorrow awaits those who argue with their Creator.
　　Does a clay pot argue with its maker?
Does the clay dispute with the one who shapes it, saying,
　　'Stop, you're doing it wrong!'
Does the pot exclaim,
　　'How clumsy can you be?'
ISAIAH 45:9

And yet, O LORD, you are our Father.
　　We are the clay, and you are the potter.

We all are formed by your hand.

ISAIAH 64:8

I personally believe God is not only bigger than cancer, He is bigger than my faith. He can heal me or anyone else on the face of this earth, with or without our great faith. God doesn't *need* anything to show His power, including just the right measure of faith.

Isn't that incredibly freeing? Doesn't that take the pressure off? Your faith doesn't have to be bigger than your cancer because God already is bigger. As believers we can trust His work in our lives.

I know Beth and Laura both felt freed knowing there wasn't something wrong with their faith or their prayers. They decided to continue to believe in miracles but ultimately to trust in Jesus alone.

If you want to know the earthly end to Beth's story—she passed away peacefully in her sleep more than *fifteen years* after her initial diagnosis and nine years after her first recurrence. She died knowing that she was going to be healed—just not in the time frame she had wished.

Josh later told me that he thought God had brought them to our town to start a new business, but he now believes it was to meet Marc and me and have our spiritual care in their lives. I am so honored that God would use us in His great plan to walk such a difficult journey with such an "ideal patient."

       ✇   ✇   ✇

Will your cancer or your loved one's cancer come back? Hopefully not, but I can't make any promises. Will my cancer come back? Hopefully not, but I have no guarantees either.

Because I work in an oncology office, almost every day I see people get the news that their cancer has returned. Realistically, I know it can happen. But I also see people whose cancer—against all odds—

does not return. I have faith that God is able to do much more than we can ask or imagine (see Ephesians 3:20).

I think of my friend Steve, a college professor diagnosed with prostate cancer at the age of forty-two, who had two more recurrences before he reached forty-five.

He started attending the Cancer Prayer Support Group shortly after the second recurrence and was trying to find that healthy balance of realism, positive attitude, and faith.

But every time he went to see his urologist for a checkup, the doctor started with the sentence, "Now you know this is terminal."

Steve found this really irritating—as if a cancer patient could ever forget that he had been told he had incurable cancer. I suggested the next time his doctor said this, Steve should smack the palm of his hand to his forehead and announce, "Silly me, I completely forgot that! Thanks so much for reminding me!" I really wanted to see what the doctor would say to that!

I also suggested to Steve that he might want to find another physician because he always felt so annoyed after seeing his present one. And that is just what Steve did. His new physician, of course, knows that Steve will always be in cancer's shadow, but she also knows she doesn't have to remind him of this fact at every visit.

It has now been fourteen years since Steve was diagnosed and eleven years since he was told his cancer was incurable. In 2004 his PSA—a blood test that shows the presence of prostate cancer—started climbing again and Steve began chemotherapy. But from 1999 to 2002 Steve enjoyed a three-year remission, during which time he changed careers and became a senior associate pastor at a very large church in our area.

"When the senior pastor asked me to apply for the position, I thought he was crazy," Steve says. "I do have cancer, you know!" he recalls telling him. "But the pastor said 'I don't think that should be a big issue.'"

"Not a big issue?" Steve recalls saying. "It's the biggest issue of my life!"

Now after serving for five years at the church, Steve realizes cancer wasn't the biggest problem in his life; it was his fear of it coming back again. "God has taught me that you don't stop living your life," he says. "There could be career changes and new opportunities in spite of the cancer."

I consider Steve another ideal patient who lives with the question of *when* his cancer will come back, not *whether* it will come back. But he also has a deep faith and knows that God has plans for his life no matter what his PSA level is.

"Even though I'm faced with this ongoing disease, God said 'that shouldn't stop you from serving Me,'" Steve says. "I don't even ask 'Why?' anymore, and I don't pray for healing. I pray that His purpose will be fulfilled in my life."

Sounds pretty ideal to me.

ᘓᘔ   ᘓᘔ   ᘓᘔ

I'd like to leave you with a little poem I wrote for my husband when we were first married. It's my word of encouragement to you as you try to become the ideal patient: trusting in God as you pray the cancer doesn't come back and trusting in Him if it does.

> *To believe in someone*
> *Is to have faith*
> *In God's ability as the Potter*
> *And in that person's willingness to be the clay.*
> *I believe in you.*

CHAPTER 11

What If I Need a Miracle?

It is tempting to say that I never met a person with cancer whom
I didn't like.

But that would be untrue.

There was one.

I have met 1,489 newly diagnosed patients in Marc's office, and
I can truthfully say I liked 1,488 of them right away. This is a story
about the one and only one I didn't like and how God did a miracle
in both our lives.

It's the story of a man who was told from the moment of his diagnosis that he always would be under cancer's shadow because he had
a medically incurable (albeit treatable) form of the disease. He was
told he could expect multiple recurrences and that the disease probably would take his life within five years. There was no hope of a cure.

What he wasn't told was that God had other plans.

If you, too, ever need a miracle, you'll love Frank's story. Even if
you don't need one, I believe you'll be blessed by the amazing way
God worked in both our lives.

I met "Frank" officially in our office in January of 1997 when
he came as a newly diagnosed patient. I knew of him already
though because his wife was our patient, and she and I had become
good friends. She had shared with me about times he was not very

supportive during her cancer journey, and those stories colored my perspective of Frank before I ever laid eyes on him.

I still can picture them that first day in our waiting room; she was trying to help him fill out his health history questionnaire and he wasn't cooperating. They were both very frustrated, but she was the one for whom I felt sorry.

I sized up Frank from a distance and wasn't crazy about what I saw. He was in his early seventies and looked as if he needed a haircut and a shave—even his fingernails were too long for my liking. I wished he had worn long sleeves to cover up the tattoo on his bicep.

I am embarrassed to say this, but I decided right then and there I didn't like him and wasn't going to be friends with him. *After all,* I consoled myself, *my job doesn't say I have to get close to everybody. I will meet him today as a new patient, be cordial to him, and that will be the end of it.*

Even then I knew in my heart that that wasn't the right response for a person claiming to love and follow God, but I continued justifying my attitude.

God, you know I've liked everybody else I've met in here. I've liked all but one. I think that's a pretty good batting average. Surely you don't expect me to bat 1.000?

When I discussed his diagnosis/prognosis later that day with Marc, I mentioned that I wasn't too excited about meeting Frank.

"Did you see the tattoo of the naked lady on his arm?" I asked with obvious displeasure.

"No," Marc replied. "I was too busy looking at the swastika on his other arm."

He laughed. Even though as a Jew the symbol was offensive to him, I could tell it wasn't going to alter the way he treated this patient.

"He probably got it a long time ago and wishes he didn't," Marc added.

I wasn't about to be that gracious but dropped the subject anyway.

The next day I dutifully sent Frank a note slightly exaggerating that it was "nice" to meet him.

Well, at least I'm done with him, I thought.

I didn't even feel bad that I had no intention of reaching out to him anymore or making any special attempts to befriend him. On the contrary, I was proud of myself for being so cordial to him.

A few months later Frank's wife passed away, and I couldn't help but wonder why he got to live and she didn't.

It wasn't long before I got my answer.

℘℘ ℘℘ ℘℘

One day in the spring of 1998, Marc took me aside and told me he was admitting Frank to the hospital because of an accidental overdose of his chemotherapy. I was very distraught to hear this—not so much about Frank as for Marc—because I knew he was upset that this could have happened. Frank took an oral chemo at home for his cancer, and through a series of errors by him, the pharmacy, and our office, he took way too much. In fact, he took a lethal dose.

"What's going to happen?" I asked Marc.

"He's going to die," he answered matter-of-factly. "I'm putting him in the hospital, but there's nothing I really can do to stop this."

Frank's white blood cell count, which should have been between 4,000 and 10,000, had plummeted to 300. Marc read all the literature about this lethal chemo dose, which predicted it would take two weeks for that count to bottom out. There was no way Frank would survive with no white cells to protect him from infection.

"Well, I'm praying that he won't die," I firmly told Marc. I think I was praying more for Marc than Frank, but it was still my prayer.

A thought flashed through my mind: *It's going to be a little difficult to keep ignoring this patient now. I'll pray for him really hard, but I am still not going to befriend him.*

A couple of days later I started to feel a little guilty (finally!) and went over to the hospital to visit Frank. It was the first time we'd had a conversation of any substance. I wasn't sure what his frame of mind might be, so I determined I would not bring up the overdose. But he did.

"I don't fault Dr. Hirsh at all," he said. "He was trying to be helpful and work with me, and it was my fault I took too many pills."

That's a relief to hear.

"I'm not going to die," he told me. "I'm going to San Diego to see my first great-grandchild born."

Not exactly realistic, but I do like your spunk, I thought.

He talked more about his family and the church he attended. I was feeling pretty small as he seemed more and more likable.

Okay, I'll pray with him, but I am not holding his hand.

"Would you like me to pray for you?" I asked as I always do beforehand so as not to offend anybody.

"Sure," he said with a big smile.

Contrary to the hundreds and hundreds of other times I've prayed with cancer patients, I did not hold his hand when I took his need before the God of the universe. We prayed—without touching—for a miracle in his life.

I stood up feeling as if I should get a medal for my exemplary behavior, and then he told me that I could come see him again.

Why did he have to say that? I was really hoping he wouldn't like me and I could just pray for him from afar.

So about a week later I went back over to the hospital. His white count, instead of waiting two weeks to bottom out, started climbing right after that first visit and was already up to 1,200— still not good, but a whole lot better.

We chatted about his wife and I could see how much he loved and missed her. I prayed with him again (still no hand-holding!) especially asking that he would feel God's amazing love for him.

I gave him a copy of my favorite booklet of encouragement, which is called "Someone Cares," and is filled with prayers and Scripture verses for those who are sick. I didn't really think he would be interested since he said he wasn't much of a reader. I looked back into the room as I left and he already was reading the first page.

I came back the next day. We talked more, we prayed more, and the white count went up more.

I came back again the following day. The conversation now was turning easily to weighty matters such as healing and dying.

"Are you afraid of dying?" I asked him.

"Nope," he told me. "Everybody has to go sometime."

"What do you think happens to people when they die?" I ventured a little further.

"You either go up or you go down," he quickly answered.

But when I pressed the issue further, Frank didn't know how our eternal destiny is decided and whether people could know for sure whether they were going "up or down."

So I shared with him what the Bible calls the Good News. It's the message that our eternal destiny is decided by whether we turn from our sins and accept the free gift of salvation offered to us by God through His Son, Jesus.

And anyone who believes in God's Son has eternal life. Anyone
who doesn't obey the Son will never experience eternal life.
JOHN 3:36

And we can know for sure whether we're headed "up or down."

But these things are written so that you may continue to believe
that Jesus is the Messiah, the Son of God, and that by believing
in him you will have life.
JOHN 20:31

It's certainly the best news I've ever heard, because if we really
are going to live forever, only a very few of those years will be here
on earth. It sure helps these days make more sense if we know where
we're going to spend the rest of our days.

I asked Frank if he wanted to pray and have that assurance of
heaven. He said yes, so I took his hand in mine—that hand with the
long fingernails on the arm with an offensive tattoo—and I prayed.

By now I could tell God was really working in Frank's life, but
I also knew He really was working in mine.

A few days later we visited at the hospital. It was now almost
three weeks since his lethal overdose, and even Marc was starting to
be cautiously optimistic that somehow against all medical evidence
and logic Frank might survive.

Frank told me that day that he loved the "Someone Cares" booklet I gave him and that he had given it to his daughter to read. He
talked freely about a lot of subjects, including his tattoos, which he
said he got many, many years ago and now regretted. (I hate it when
Marc is right!)

At the end of our time I asked him if he wanted to pray—still
thinking I wouldn't have to hold his hand this time because I had

done it the last time! But immediately he held his hand out to me. He
wanted to hold my hand. Me, the rotten patient advocate who was
determined not to be his friend. Here was the kind patient reaching
out to me.

I didn't deserve such love.

I, who loved to share the Good News that "God demonstrates his
own love for us in this: While we were still sinners, Christ died for
us" (Romans 5:8, NIV), was experiencing what it felt like to receive
undeserved love.

Frank asked me to pray that he could quit smoking and for him
to grow closer to God. We held hands long after the prayer and I
savored the moment as God filled my heart with more love for Him,
and more importantly, a new love for Frank.

A couple of days later Frank's white count was high enough for
him to get out of the hospital, and he soon came to our office for a
recheck. His hair was cut, his face was clean-shaven, and even his
nails were shorter! He was smiling when he saw me, and he gave me
a big hug.

Everybody in the office was all abuzz. "What happened to Frank?"
they kept asking.

The funny thing was that although only Frank looked different
on the outside, I knew we were both very different on the inside.

Over the next few weeks, Frank was in the office often and
always had a hug and a kiss on the cheek for me. I looked forward
to seeing him each time because he was such an incredible reminder
of God's unconditional love and His miraculous power even when
there is "no hope."

A month later, true to his word, Frank left for San Diego to visit
his daughter and meet his first great-grandchild, whom he got to
hold the day after he was born. When he returned home after a

two-month visit, he said he felt wonderful, and medical tests showed him in complete remission from his cancer. We even got to the point of joking that he'd discovered a "cure" for his medically incurable cancer!

Frank quit smoking early in 1999, a long-awaited answer to our prayer, although lingering respiratory problems continued to plague him from his years with the addiction.

One of the last times I saw Frank before he moved to San Diego for good was in the spring of 1999 when he was in the hospital for treatment of his emphysema. We talked about all God had done in his life and the miracle of his recovery after the overdose. We prayed together for him to keep his faith, hope, and trust in Jesus alone and thanked God for the assurance he would one day "go up."

There were tears in Frank's eyes as we both knew he had done nothing to "deserve" a miracle from God. But there were more tears in my eyes because I knew all too well that I did not deserve anything God had done for me either.

Frank's miracle was a free gift—one that neither of us understood but both of us treasured.

I believe that just as we can't earn our salvation, we can't earn a physical healing. Whether you or your loved one lives or dies is ultimately up to God. If you pray for a physical healing, rejoice if it comes, but don't imagine it was an answer to just the right prayer or good deed.

And if you pray for a physical healing and it doesn't seem to be coming, please don't torture yourself with the thought that there was something else you could or should have done. Healing isn't something we wrench from God's hand. It's a gift freely given as God wills. And if someone ever tells you that there's no medical hope, that you need a miracle, remember Frank.

After his move to the West Coast to be with family, he lived several more years without taking another drop of chemotherapy, and he remained cancer-free until his death at the age of seventy-nine.

But, of course, that's only the end of Frank's story here on earth. For I expect when I get to heaven he'll be waiting for me with a hug and a kiss on the cheek. I know there are no tears in heaven, but it's hard to imagine that the sight of us there together won't make me cry.

CHAPTER 12

Is God *Really* Bigger Than Cancer?

Sometimes you hear people say there isn't anything God can't do. But that's not really true.

God definitely knows all, hears all, and sees all. He is even all-powerful, but that doesn't mean there aren't some things that He can't do.

For instance:

- He can't sin. (1 Peter 1:16, Revelation 15:4)
- He can't lie. (Psalm 89:35, Romans 3:4)
- He can't fail to keep His promises. (Hebrews 10:23)
- He can't allow anything in this world to separate His followers from His love. (Romans 8:38-39)

In fact, God can't do anything that is inconsistent with His unchanging character. So if you get to know God really well—you know, up-close-and-personal—you will see all that He can do and therefore some things He cannot.

One of the things that I believe with all my heart is that God *can* heal cancer. Why do I believe it? Because the Bible tells us that He is a healing God. In Exodus 15:26, God announces, "I am the LORD who heals you." The Old Testament writers call Him Yahweh Raphe, the God who heals.

One of the ways Jesus proved that He was the long-awaited Messiah was by healing people (Matthew 4:23). He healed people by touching them, speaking to them, and even spitting on them (see Mark 8:23, Mark 7:33, and John 9:6)! One lady just barely touched His robe's tzitzit (the fringes at the bottom) and she was miraculously healed. Everywhere He went crowds gathered, and He healed the blind, the deaf, and the lame.

Could you imagine the uproar if Jesus walked into Sloan-Kettering or Johns Hopkins or any cancer center today? There would be a real "feeding frenzy" of cancer patients wanting to get close to Him.

I have been a patient advocate for more than a decade, and I have touched and prayed for God's healing touch on hundreds of cancer patients, but there has only been one time that I felt that an instantaneous healing took place. I'd like to tell you the story, partly because of what happened, but especially because of what *didn't* happen.

        ❧❧   ❧❧   ❧❧

My encounter with Jim started with one of those desperate pleas I sometimes get from the nurses at our local hospital. The requests usually center on a cancer patient who is really having a hard time emotionally or spiritually, and the busy nurses simply don't have the time to give the patient the extra attention he or she needs. So they ask if I would visit with that patient.

"Do you remember Mrs. Gaffga?" a nurse asked me as I was about to pass her in the fourth-floor hallway.

"Sure, I remember her," I responded. "She was our patient but passed away from ovarian cancer a couple of months ago."

"That's right," the nurse continued. "Well, her husband is on the floor waiting to be taken down for a CT-guided biopsy. He's a smoker and has lesions throughout his lung. And the really bad part is his middle school–aged son is there in the room, and he's really freaking out because his mom already died from cancer and now he's afraid his dad is also going to die," she added. "Will you go and see them?"

"Sure, I'd be glad to," I responded half-truthfully.

The "sure" part was true—I would definitely go because it's my job to offer emotional and spiritual support to cancer patients and their families.

The "I'd be glad to" part definitely was a stretch. I was never crazy about walking into the room of a stranger in distress because I never assumed the person would be happy to meet me (remember Eric in chapter 8?). I especially wasn't thrilled about walking into the room of a distressed stranger with a distraught young boy.

To top it all off, one of the reasons I remembered Jim's wife so well—besides the fact that she died of cancer at only thirty-five—was that on her health-history questionnaire she indicated she had no religion and her spiritual faith was not at all important to her. It was very easy to remember patients who responded as she did because she was one of only a very few who had given those negative responses. When I see that combination of answers I consider it a red light concerning discussions of spiritual matters.

I had only met her husband, Jim, once in our office and had no knowledge of whether he had any spiritual beliefs. I was going to assume a red light concerning faith discussions with him unless he told me otherwise.

Not being able to talk about God or pray didn't leave me with a lot to do, but I headed to Jim's room, whispering a silent prayer as I walked down the hospital corridor. I felt a little encouraged that I

could at least try to talk to and comfort his son while he waited
for his dad to have the biopsy done.

But when I got to the room, Jim's son had gotten so upset he
had left.

*Perfect. Now I am alone with a distressed stranger who probably
doesn't want to talk about God or pray,* I thought. *This should be a quick
visit.*

I gingerly tiptoed toward the lone bed and reintroduced myself
to Jim. Thankfully he remembered meeting me at Marc's and said it
was all right for me to visit with him. We made a little small talk and
then chatted about his wife. I could see the pain of losing her was far
worse than any fear of his own possible cancer.

Finally we talked about him. Jim said the suspicious lesions had
been spotted on a routine chest X-ray. A lung specialist explained to
him that he needed to biopsy the area to see if any cancer could be
found. (This is done by taking a CT scan during the procedure so the
technician can guide the needle to the right spot where tissue is withdrawn and sampled for cancer cells.) The specialist further explained
to Jim that just because the biopsies came back negative, cancer
could not be ruled out. The next step would be to go in surgically
and remove additional tissue that could be examined under the
microscope for a more definite pathology.

Bottom line, Jim wasn't going to get good news today: Either he
did have cancer or he needed a more invasive, riskier test to rule it
out. I could see the fear in his eyes—partly for himself but mainly for
his two children, the older of whom I knew was not handling the situation well. I, of course, was powerless to do anything about these
desperate circumstances, but I knew God was not. Very timidly
I asked Jim if I might say a prayer for him. He seemed so out of
options I figured it was worth a try. Without hesitation, Jim said yes.

Now you know from Frank's story that normally I like to hold someone's hand when I pray with that person, but I am extremely careful never to put myself in compromising situations with men. Jim was just a few years younger than I, and we were alone in a room with the door closed. That made me feel nervous about any hand-holding.

And then God spoke to my heart: *Put your hand on his lung and pray.*

You've got to be kidding. I'm worried about sending the wrong signal by holding his hand and you want me to put my hand on his lung with nothing but a flimsy hospital gown between me and his bare chest? That sounds like a really bad idea!

Put your hand on his lung and pray.

This is making me really uncomfortable.

Trust Me.

So I garnered my courage and asked Jim if I might place my hand on his lung where the suspicious spots were and pray for him. He agreed.

I spread out the fingers on my right hand and ever so lightly placed my hand on his chest and I prayed that God would touch and heal and show him His mighty power. It was a short prayer and I didn't feel anything happen when I prayed, but Jim's eyes and mine were teary when I finished.

When I got back to the office I told Marc right away what had happened—especially the part about me laying my hand on Jim's chest.

"You know I don't usually do that, especially with single men I don't know," I quickly explained, feeling somehow like a kid who's been caught with her hand in the cookie jar. "I hope it was all right. I just felt like God told me to do it."

"I'm sure it was fine," Marc said, not even looking up from his paperwork.

Then just to see if he was really listening, I added, "Don't worry, I'm not going to start laying hands on all the men I pray for—especially not the prostate cancers."

He looked up and gave me a grin: "I'm not worried."

☙☙   ☙☙   ☙☙

I figured I would call Jim a couple of days later to see what the CT scan showed.

But the very next day a dozen long-stemmed red roses were delivered to my office. I knew they weren't from my husband, because although he is wonderful about buying me flowers for special anniversaries, he knows I would not be happy if he spent the money to have a bouquet like that delivered!

I held my breath and looked at the card: "Thanks for the lovely prayer. You're a lovely lady. Jim."

Oh no, he did get the wrong idea. What am I going to do now?

I knew I had to set the record straight quickly with Jim but thought I better find out what happened with his test first. I called the office of the specialist who was scheduled to do the biopsies. Thankfully this was before all the restrictive patient privacy laws went into effect and I could get a little information.

"How did Jim's CT-guided biopsy come out yesterday?" I asked the secretary, who knew me from Marc's office.

"He didn't have a biopsy," she responded.

"Oh yes, he did," I said trying not to sound like she didn't know what she was talking about.

"No, he didn't," she repeated firmly.

"Yes, he did," I countered. "I was there with him yesterday at the hospital. He was all prepped, and I stayed with him until they took him down for the biopsy."

"Well, he didn't have one," she said. "When they did the CT scan, the lesions were shrunk so much the doctor said there was no way they were cancer. He canceled the biopsy."

The roses were beginning to make a little more sense.

I called Jim and left a message on his machine thanking him for the beautiful flowers but making it clear that it was God who healed him and not me. I dropped a card and little book of prayers in the mail to him, hoping that he might want to pray on his own.

A couple of days later I got an e-mail from him thanking me for my correspondence and mentioning my "healing powers." I now knew Jim wasn't confused about my feelings for him, but I wasn't sure he understood God's feelings for him.

I decided to stick my neck out and write Jim a note explaining what God really had done in his life and why.

"God has touched you and healed you physically, but He has so much more He wants to do in your life," I told him. "He has a lot more healing in store for you. He wants to heal you spiritually so that even when you eventually do die you will live forever with Him."

I knew God had done a physical miracle in Jim's life so that his heart might be softened enough to receive a spiritual miracle—the best kind of miracle because the cure for sin (a spiritual sickness) outlasts any cure for cancer (a physical sickness).

I'm not sure if Jim ever believed that God healed him; he never said so to me. I hope and pray that his physical miracle was the beginning and not the end of God's work in his life.

It's true that no matter how many times any of us beat cancer or get a miracle, we still are going to die someday. That's why whatever happens to us physically on this earth is of far less consequence than what happens to us spiritually. The former has temporary results; the latter has eternal consequences.

I wish I had a zillion stories to tell you about people I've prayed over who instantly were healed. I'm sure doing so would sell a lot more copies of this book. I know there are books out there that *promise* cures for cancer. I can promise you that they are preying on desperate people and that I know many people who have tried such "cures" without success.

Many times I, too, have wished for a cure for cancer. In my job, I see many cancer patients cured through treatment, but I also see many who aren't cured. Many times my heart cries out to God: *Why don't you heal?*

I sometimes feel like the man Job in the Bible who saw a lot of suffering—he lost his livestock, his servants, his children, and his own health—and he wondered where God was in the midst of it all. I never received a logical explanation to my healing questions, just as Job didn't get one to the question of his own sufferings.

God's very long answer to Job basically says: "When you can create the entire world and keep everything running in order, then you can ask Me questions about why I allowed you to suffer." (You can read God's actual words in Job chapters 38–41.)

Job's humble response was this: "I know that you can do anything, and no one can stop you. . . . I was talking about things I did not understand, things far too wonderful for me" (Job 42:2-3, NLT-1).

⊘ ⊘ ⊘

I've felt a little like Job over the years as I've dedicated my life to praying for and with cancer patients and their families. So many times I've prayed but haven't seen God show up in the way I knew He could and hoped He would.

I never said it out loud, but in my mind sometimes I wondered: *Are You really bigger than cancer?*

I'd like to share with you one more story so you can see how God answered that question for me in a most unusual way.

The incident happened in March 2004 when a group of staff and spouses from my church attended a Tuesday evening prayer service at the Brooklyn Tabernacle in Brooklyn, New York. This huge, multiracial congregation has become well-known because of the writings of its pastor Jim Cymbala and its phenomenal choir led by his composer-wife, Carol.

I recently had read *Fresh Wind, Fresh Fire*, his book about the power of prayer, and wanted to visit the prayer service to see it for myself. My husband had been there twice and raved about the worship, the prayers, and the powerful sense of God's presence.

About a dozen of us spent the day sightseeing in New York and then after dinner headed to the Tabernacle, where we joined about two thousand others for the midweek prayer meeting.

The service was indeed wonderful: the music uplifting, the preaching inspiring, and the prayers very powerful as we joined voices with so many who didn't look like us. It reminded me of a little microcosm of what heaven will be like when people from every tribe and tongue and nation join together and worship the same God (see Revelation 7:9).

Yet I remember thinking that while it was a wonderful prayer meeting, it was not a real "spiritual high" for me. I have been at much bigger faith meetings. I've listened to fantastic preaching with five thousand Christian leaders from around the world at Willow Creek Community Church, sung with twenty thousand ladies at Women of

Faith conferences, and worshipped with forty-five thousand others at outdoor Creation music festivals. Brooklyn Tabernacle was extremely uplifting, but I didn't feel the service had been a mountaintop experience for me.

Near the end of the service Pastor Cymbala surprised us by saying he had heard there was a pastor and his staff and their spouses visiting from Pennsylvania, and he invited us to come down front for prayer. (We later found out that one of the men in our group had called ahead and asked that we might have this special opportunity.)

We excitedly went forward to the stage area where ushers moved us front and center in the ornate former Broadway theater. My husband and I and our associate pastor and his wife were smack dab in the middle on ground level right below the podium. Pastor Cymbala called for others to come forward if they wanted prayer and soon it was standing room only in the altar area.

Several leaders from the congregation came out onstage and leaned down and began to pray over us in the front row. A gentleman placed his hands on my husband's shoulder and prayed for us. I couldn't hear his words but felt joy at being prayed for by a total stranger.

I continued to stand holding hands with my husband on my left and holding my right hand palm up in an attitude of prayer. A few moments passed and soon I felt someone take hold of my right hand.

I peeked.

It was Jim Cymbala!

The Jim Cymbala who wrote all those best sellers.

Jim Cymbala was kneeling down and praying over me!

My heart was racing. I knew he could "really pray" and I wanted to tell him what to pray for me. A little conversation began in my head. Tell him about your ministry to cancer patients. Ask him to pray for them. I had been praying silently to God about just that topic when Pastor Cymbala knelt by me.

But then reality hit.

God hears you when you pray for your ministry to cancer patients.

You don't need Jim Cymbala to get your message to God.

Tell Him what's on your heart yourself.

So I did. I poured out my heart about how frustrated I feel when I pray for patients and they still die and how hard it is to see so much suffering. I asked him to inspire me to write this book, which at that time I was calling *God Is Bigger than Cancer.*

Within moments Pastor Cymbala moved on. (I didn't peek this time so I can't say where he went.) Soon a tall man appeared (obviously I peeked a little then) and he, too, leaned down for prayer. But instead of putting his hand on my husband's shoulder as the other gentleman had done, he cupped the fingers of his left hand and ever so gently touched his fingertips to the center of my forehead. The touch was so light I could barely feel it. But within seconds I began to feel it elsewhere.

My arms started shaking, my legs felt very weak, and I had the sensation that everyone in the front row was rocking back and forth. And then it hit me: *I am going down.*

Because you've gotten this far in the book, I think you have a pretty good idea that I'm not a real emotional person. I'm a skeptical former newspaper reporter at heart and I always need the facts. So my mind started spitting out "facts."

You could hurt your back if you go down.

You don't really believe in this kind of stuff.

This is going to be embarrassing.

And then I heard one more Voice: *Don't fight it.*

So I stopped arguing in my mind and let my body do what it

seemed to want to do—fall down in front of two thousand people. My husband later told me that both he and the man praying for me tried to hold me up but there was no stopping the fall.

And so I fell onto the carpeted floor and on top of the feet of the people behind me who weren't able to get out of the way quickly enough. My husband said he tried to get one woman to move back but she replied, "I can't—she's on top of my foot!"

I have no idea how long I was lying there—only that time didn't seem to matter. I was filled with joy and I could pray without my mind doing its usual wandering. So that's what I did. I lay on the floor with tears of joy streaming down my face and my lips moving in silent prayer. Nothing hurt, including my back and its one-time compressed disc!

After a while, my husband helped me up and we started to walk out. My legs felt like rubber and I had to lean on his arm. Those from my church who saw what had happened were in shock because they knew I wasn't one to fake something like this.

Still bewildered that this could happen to *me*, I felt a little less strange knowing that many others must have felt God's power as I did.

So I asked my husband, "Did you go down too?"

"No," he replied.

"Did a lot of people go down?"

"No."

"Did *anyone* else go down?"

"No, you were the only one." (And you thought God didn't have a sense of humor!)

I don't want to get into a theological dissertation of what happened. I know some people call such incidents "being slain in the Spirit." I never liked that term because it sounded like the Holy Spirit was killing somebody. I met author-priest Francis MacNutt one time and he talked about "resting in the Spirit"—when God touches somebody and that person just rests in Him while He works in his or her life.

That is much more how I would describe what happened to me. I felt as if I was resting in God. As I reflected on that night and what God wanted to say to me, it was as if He was answering my ever-present question by saying: *So you want to see if I'm bigger than cancer? Watch this.*

And then He touched me and knocked all the skepticism out of me without giving me any facts except this one: *I am very BIG and you are very small.*

Like Job, it was all I needed to know.

CHAPTER 13

Living under a Different Shadow

There I was staring right into the steely eyes of a hammerhead shark. Then another shark swam toward me. Over my shoulder, I could see a third heading my way.

I never flinched. I didn't even attempt to run. In fact, I thoroughly enjoyed the whole experience.

Why? Not because I still have chemo-brain and didn't remember that sharks can be very dangerous. No, it was because I was completely protected from them.

The experience took place at the aquarium in Baltimore's Inner Harbor, and I was standing on dry ground watching the menacing-looking sharks swim past me in a huge, wraparound glass saltwater tank. They couldn't have touched me even if they had wanted to. So you see, it is possible to be surrounded by something life-threatening and yet feel very safe!

There's no arguing that cancer is a life-threatening disease—fatal for half the people diagnosed with it. The shadow it casts on survivors and loved ones can at times seem very menacing.

In grade-school science, you may have learned that a shadow is caused by the absence of light when an opaque (not see-through) object has absorbed the light. When cancer becomes a shadow in our lives, I believe it's blocking the light from reaching us. That's why I've

shared all these true stories about cancer patients and their families—
so you can believe that we truly can find the light despite cancer's
shadow.

Another truth about shadows is that they fall *opposite* their light
source. That's why your shadow is in front of you if the sun is behind
you and vice versa. The way we're facing determines whether or not
we can see the shadow easily.

Not being a rocket scientist (or even very good in science), I just
stopped writing and went outside to double-check that this is correct. I stood in my driveway facing a beautiful, bright ball of sun and
I could not see my shadow. Then I turned my back to the sun—still
hoping my neighbor was too busy mowing to see me doing a childish
science experiment in the driveway!—and there was my big, black
shadow clearly visible right in front of me.

I know this is a simple scientific fact, but it is a profound spiritual truth for us cancer survivors and our loved ones. We have to
keep facing the light in order not to see cancer's shadow so easily.
We must keep turned in the right direction.

Do you remember in 1998 when the Galaxy IV communications
satellite malfunctioned and rotated out of position, turning away
from the earth? In an instant millions of pagers went silent, TV and
radio stations couldn't transmit, and even some gas pumps couldn't
accept credit cards. It all happened because just one satellite in the
heavens turned the wrong way and couldn't communicate with
earth.

Perhaps when you first heard the diagnosis of cancer you got
out of position spiritually. You couldn't figure out how a loving God
could allow cancer into your life. Maybe you even felt at times as if
He didn't hear your prayers. I hope you will check to see which way
you are facing now. I believe the way to communicate with God is to

be turned toward Him, pouring out our hearts to the One who hears, understands, and has the power to respond.

Once we're facing Him, talking to Him, and listening to Him, we also can *choose to live under a different shadow.* Now I know it sounds strange that you could find light by being *under* a shadow, but it's true.

The shadow I want you to move under—or stay under if you're already there—is a much, much bigger shadow than cancer's shadow. It's a safe, secure, protective shadow. There's no other shadow that can eclipse this one. And underneath it, we're not in the dark; we're supernaturally in the light. You see, while the Bible describes God as light, it also refers to Him as a shadow, protecting us in His shade.

> *Those who live in the shelter of the Most High*
> *will find rest in the shadow of the Almighty.*
> PSALM 91:1

The shadow of the Almighty.

I love that word picture. In my mind's eye I see myself with a little dark cancer cloud over my head moving under the huge shadow of God Himself. Standing underneath Him, it's so bright that I can barely even see the little shadow-speck of cancer.

Have you ever put your arms around a child and drawn him close to you, protecting him from the rain and the noise? Have you ever seen a mother hen spread her wings and gather her little chicks to safety as a bigger bird approached? That's the picture that the Bible gives us of God's love and care for us.

> *How precious is your unfailing love, O God!*
> *All humanity finds shelter*
> *in the shadow of your wings.*
> PSALM 36:7

Keep me as the apple of your eye;
hide me in the shadow of your wings.
PSALM 17:8 (NIV)

He has hidden me in the shadow of his hand.
ISAIAH 49:2

Let me live forever in your sanctuary,
safe beneath the shelter of your wings!
PSALM 61:4

Because you are my help,
I sing in the shadow of your wings.
My soul clings to you;
your right hand upholds me.
PSALM 63:7-8 (NIV)

Of course God the Father, who is Spirit, doesn't have real flesh-and-blood wings, but He is able to protect us by His awesome power.

I loved watching my friend Carollynn live under the shadow of the Almighty. She lived eight years and two months cancer-free after her diagnosis of a brain tumor and another seven months free-of-cancer until she went Home.

Carollynn's favorite Bible verse was Psalm 91:4.

He will cover you with his feathers.
He will shelter you with his wings.
His faithful promises are your armor and protection.

It was the verse God prompted Carollynn to read when she was first diagnosed with cancer in January 1995 at the age of forty-six. It gave her incredible hope and started a real fascination with "feathers" and the number 914.

"Whenever I see a feather it reminds me of God's protection for me," she told me shortly after moving to the area and joining my support group. "And I like to look for the number 914 on signs to remind me of God's constant care for me."

I had to chuckle when Carollynn's first grandchild was born on her birthday and weighed 9 pounds, 14 ounces! When Carollynn passed away just a few months later at 4:19 p.m., her husband, Ed, said he had to smile at what he felt was a last gift from Carollynn to remind him of her special verse. "One final example of her fabulous humor," he wrote in an e-mail to friends and family.

Some of Carollynn's amazing life under God's wings was told in a children's book called *Sea Feather*, named after the first of many wild ponies she purchased on Chincoteague Island and donated to deserving children. More of her "feather-filled" life was shared in a video that aired on the television network *Animal Planet* in November 2003, just a month after her passing. (The nonprofit Feather Fund has been established to continue her work of donating wild ponies to children.)[17] When I see feathers today, they remind me of my beautiful friend Carollynn and how she lived free-of-cancer. But they also remind me of my God whose "wings" protect me from cancer's shadow.

๏   ๏   ๏

Can you feel those wings over you—protecting you, shielding you, drawing you close? Have you trusted God enough to truly let Him cover you? He longs to do that for you.

How often I have wanted to gather your children together as a hen protects her chicks beneath her wings, but you wouldn't let me.
Jesus speaking in MATTHEW 23:37

Do you know Him well enough to truly trust Him? He longs
to have that kind of personal relationship with you.

My heart has heard you say, "Come and talk with me."
And my heart responds, "LORD, I am coming."
PSALM 27:8

The more I get to know some people, the harder it is to trust
them. But the more I've gotten to know Jesus, the more I trust
Him. I knew *about* Jesus for many years before I *really* knew Him
personally.

I know when we meet a famous person, we are sometimes disappointed that he or she doesn't seem quite as awesome up close as
from a distance. When I was a senior in high school I sat right next to
Roy Rogers in church and just thought he was some old farmer with
a really good singing voice!

But I promise that as you draw closer to God—the more you get
under the shadow of the Almighty—you will not be disappointed. In
fact, God isn't as great as we imagined He would be—He's even greater.

Yours, O LORD, is the greatness, the power, the glory, the victory,
and the majesty. Everything in the heavens and on earth is yours,
O LORD. . . . We adore you as the one who is over all things.
1 CHRONICLES 29:11

But anyone who believes in him will not be disappointed.
ROMANS 9:33 (NLT-1)

Every day I talk with disappointed people. One person is disappointed because the cancer has returned after five years. Another is
disappointed because she's going to lose her hair. Still another is disappointed that the hormone pill is not working.

But I also talk to people who have trusted in the Lord and are not disappointed.

"I didn't think I ever would say this, but it was a blessing to have cancer," Jutta wrote me in an e-mail recently. "God knew what I needed in order to grow closer to Him and understand Him better. How much God has blessed me through all of this!"

Keep in mind that those words are coming from a woman diagnosed with the deadliest kind of cancer—a woman living in a very dark shadow who has found a very great light. You, too, can live in that light.

> *The people who walk in darkness will see a great light—a light that will shine on all who live in the land where death casts its shadow.*
>
> ISAIAH 9:2 (NLT-1)

Now I know that this verse is a prophecy talking about the coming of Messiah hundreds of years before Jesus was born, but I also think it applies to us cancer survivors and our loved ones. We are people living in a land where death casts its shadow, and we need to see a great light.

My friend Mary is another survivor who found a great light in cancer's very big shadow on her life. She lost her husband to cancer and then a few years later at the age of sixty-seven was diagnosed with cancer herself. She was given only a 20 percent chance of survival.

Living with the fear of recurrence was controlling her life for quite some time until about two years after her diagnosis when she wrote me this letter:

> *I realize I had wrapped myself so tightly around my cancer that I couldn't free my mind from thoughts of it. . . . In January I gave it all to*

God and asked Him to fill my heart and mind with Him and others and to replace my worrying thoughts with more meaningful things. I determined as much as possible not to speak or think of cancer for six months.

God has worked so beautifully. In addition to the volunteer work I had been doing with second grade, I'm volunteering at the local hospital and for the monthly newsletter. (I think my gift is shuffling papers!) I've also started a little "Lend an Ear" project making telephone calls to widows and older seniors who don't have much emotional support—just to give them time to talk to someone.

I don't have time now to dwell on what might or might not happen to me.

☙☙   ☙☙   ☙☙

There's an old proverb that says you can live three weeks without food, three days without water, three minutes without air, and three seconds without hope. We always find hope—and therefore life—when we live under the light of a different shadow.

> *I pray that God, the source of hope, will fill you completely with joy and peace because you trust in him. Then you will overflow with confident hope through the power of the Holy Spirit.*
> ROMANS 15:13

Would you believe that I've prayed for you even though I probably will never know your name? I have. Many times.

I prayed God would direct people to pick up this book so He might encourage them. I prayed that even if we never meet that you still would meet God and that He would meet your deepest needs.

It's the same thing I prayed for my first book, and I've heard many incredible stories of how this came true. Some people have even tracked me down and written or called to tell me amazing things that happened to them when they were reading it. A handful even drove hours to visit my cancer support group just to see if we really laugh as much as I said we did!

I also pray that you and your loved ones' bodies remain cancer-free as mine has, but more importantly I pray that you and your loved ones' minds and spirits remain free-of-cancer.

I really enjoy listening to the Dave Ramsey radio talk show on financial advice. Ramsey preaches a message of living debt-free, and when people reach that coveted pinnacle he urges them to call in to the show and scream on air at the top of their lungs: "I'm debt free!!!"

I'd love to see a similar show for those cancer survivors who've gotten good test results or had successful surgery to call in and holler, "I'm cancer-free!!!"

But my hope and my prayer is that *all* of us cancer survivors and our loved ones could call up and proclaim, "I'm free-of-cancer!!!"

To me, living in the shadow of the Almighty is the secret to finding the light in cancer's shadow. It means trusting the Almighty to keep our minds, our hearts, and our souls, free-of-cancer—whether or not our bodies are.

Cancer does not occupy my mind.
    It is seized with God's perfect peace.
Cancer has no place in my heart.
    It is filled with God's awesome love.
Cancer cannot touch my soul.
    It is saved by God's amazing grace.

I am free-of-cancer.

"A much-needed resource for those living in the shadow of this life-threatening disease" HAROLD G. KOENIG, MD

LYNN EIB

FINDING
THE LIGHT
IN CANCER'S
SHADOW

Hope,
Humor, and
Healing
after
Treatment

FREE Discussion Guide for
Finding the Light in Cancer's Shadow!

A discussion guide written by
Lynn Eib is available at

ChristianBookGuides.com

WEB-BASED RESOURCES

Author's Web site: "Equipping to Encourage"
http://www.CancerPatientAdvocate.com

Lynn Eib offers information on finding or starting a faith-based cancer support group; becoming a patient advocate; and the relationship of faith and medicine. The site also carries her column, "Word to the Weary," a list of other helpful resources, and articles by medical oncologist, Dr. Marc Hirsh.

Dave Dravecky's Outreach of Hope
13840 Gleneagle Drive
Colorado Springs, CO 80921
800-295-5880
http://www.OutreachOfHope.org
E-mail: info@outreachofhope.org

This Christian-based organization is dedicated to encouraging cancer patients, amputees, and their families. Outreach is headed by Dave Dravecky, the former major league pitcher who lost his pitching arm to cancer in 1990. Outreach publishes the free magazine, *The Encourager*, three times a year. It also offers other resources, such as the *NIV Encouragement Bible*, which has devotions and special helps for those going through difficult times.

Kids Konnected
27071 Cabot Rd. Suite #102
Laguna Hills, CA 92653
800-899-2866
http://www.KidsKonnected.org
E-mail: info@kidskonnected.org

Kids Konnected provides friendship, understanding, education, and support for kids who have a parent with cancer. It offers a twenty-four-hour hotline, a free Teddy Bear Outreach program, an online chat room, and other resources.

National Cancer Institute Office of Cancer Survivorship
Division of Cancer Control and Population Sciences
6130 Executive Boulevard
Executive Plaza North
Rockville, MD 20852
800-4-CANCER
http://www.survivorship.cancer.gov

Established in 1996 in response to the large number of people now surviving cancer for a long time, this organization is dedicated to enhancing the length and quality of life for cancer survivors and their families. The site has information on such things as research findings and telephone workshops, as well as links to post-treatment resources.

National Coalition for Cancer Survivorship
1010 Wayne Avenue
Suite 770
Silver Spring, MD 20910
301-650-9127
http://www.cansearch.org

The oldest survivor-led advocacy organization (founded in 1986), the National Coalition for Cancer Survivorship works on behalf of people with all types of cancer as well as their families. The site has information on new drugs, cancer research, health-related legislation, cancer-related conferences, and other survivorship issues.

Rest Ministries
P.O. Box 502928
San Diego, CA 92150
888-751-REST
http://www.RestMinistries.org

Rest Ministries, Inc. is a nonprofit Christian organization serving people with chronic illness or pain, as well as their families, by providing spiritual, emotional, relational, and practical support through a variety of resources, including *HopeKeepers* magazine, Bible studies, and small group materials. HopeKeepers support group/Bible studies are designed to meet the emotional and spiritual needs of people living with chronic illness or pain.

Cross Search Directory
http://www.CrossSearch.com

This is an online directory of Christian-based Web sites that can be accessed by entering a category or a keyword, such as *health* or *illness*. Users must rely on their own discretion.

Cancer Patients Christian Online Support Group
http://listserv.acor.org/archives/cpcos.html

This site features links to many online cancer support and information resources. Once registered, users can also join an online support group.

Faith & Coping with Cancer Discussion List
http://listserv.acor.org/archives/faith.html

This site is similar to the one mentioned above; however, its resources directly relate to faith and coping with cancer.

RECOMMENDED READING ON A BIBLICAL VIEW OF ILLNESS AND HEALING

Believe in Miracles, but Trust in Jesus by Adrian Rogers (Crossway Books, 1997). A study of the seven miracles recorded in the Gospel of John, which shows that the purpose of every miracle is to set our sights on the real answer to our needs: Jesus.

A Bend in the Road by David Jeremiah (Word Publishing, 2000). Drawing on ten well-loved psalms, cancer survivor/author/pastor Dr. David Jeremiah shares how to experience God when your world caves in.

Cancer: A Medical and Spiritual Guide for Patients and Their Families by William A. Fintel and Gerald R. McDermott (Baker Books, 2004). Written by a medical oncologist and a theologian, this book offers relevant and encouraging advice on coping with cancer medically, emotionally, financially, and spiritually.

Coping with Cancer by John Packo (Christian Publications, 1991). A pastor and cancer survivor shares twelve creative choices cancer patients can make to fight cancer, beginning with the affirmation "I did not choose cancer, but

I choose to trust God for courage to cope with it." The book provides an extremely balanced look at roles of conventional therapies and spiritual resources.

Disappointment with God by Philip Yancey (Zondervan Publishing, 1988). A powerful treatise on suffering that answers three questions posed by sufferers: Is God unfair? Is God silent? Is God hidden?

God, Medicine & Miracles by Daniel E. Fountain (Harold Shaw Publishers, 1999). This missionary doctor shares real-life stories (most about his work with AIDS patients in Africa) and insightful studies to help readers develop a balanced relationship between faith, medicine, and ultimate spiritual hope.

The Healing Power of a Christian Mind by William Backus (Bethany House Publishers, 1996). A psychologist discusses how biblical truth can keep people healthy.

If God Is So Good, Why Do I Hurt So Bad? by David Biebel (Revell, 1995). This book discusses suffering and God's part in it based on the two seemingly contradictory premises that "sometimes life is agony" and "our loving God is in control."

Israel's Divine Healer by Michael Brown (Zondervan Publishing, 1995). A complete and systematic look at God as the Divine Healer throughout the Old and New Testaments. Written by a Messianic Jewish scholar.

Life Is Tough, but God Is Faithful by Sheila Walsh (Thomas Nelson Publishers, 1999). Encouraging insight into God's presence in the midst of our questions and struggles.

New Light on Depression: Help, Hope, and Answers for the Depressed and Those Who Love Them by David B. Biebel and Harold G. Koenig (Zondervan Publishing, 2004). A medically reliable and biblically sound guide to finding faith and strength in the midst of depression.

A Path through Suffering by Elisabeth Elliot (Servant Publications, 1990). This book explores the relationship between God's mercy and our pain. Elliot is an author, former missionary, and Bible translator whose first husband was murdered and whose second husband died from cancer.

The Problem of Pain by C. S. Lewis (HarperSanFrancisco, 2001). This book answers the universal question: "Why would an all-loving, all-knowing God allow people to experience pain and suffering?"

When God & Cancer Meet: True Stories of Hope and Healing by Lynn Eib (Tyndale House Publishers, 2002). Eighteen real-life stories of God's amazing touch in the lives (body, mind and spirit) of cancer patients and their families, as well as a chapter on oncologist Dr. Marc Hirsh's spiritual journey that led him to become a Messianic Jew.

When God Doesn't Heal Now by Larry Keefauver (Thomas Nelson Publishers, 2000). This well-balanced book sheds biblical clarity on dangerous myths about healing that can sabotage faith and erode hope. It explains how to walk by faith while facing pain, suffering, or death, and how God is a healing God even though His timeframe may not always fit ours.

When God Doesn't Make Sense by James Dobson (Tyndale House, 1993). An immensely practical book for those struggling with trials and heartaches they can't understand, helping them to see that God is not betraying them in their time of need.

When God Says No by Leith Anderson (Bethany House Publishers, 1996). Discovering the God of Hope behind the answer we'd rather not hear. A thorough, biblical probe of the great mysteries of prayer.

When God Weeps by Joni Eareckson Tada and Steve Estes (Zondervan Publishing House, 1997). Tada, a quadriplegic since 1967, and Estes, a pastor, tackle tough questions about hardship and why God allows suffering.

Where Is God When It Hurts? by Philip Yancey (Zondervan Publishing, 1990). A thought-provoking look at the hard questions believers ask when suffering and trials come.

Why Me? A Doctor Looks at the Book of Job by Diane Komp (InterVarsity Press, 2001). A Yale professor of pediatric oncology tackles the painful questions of suffering by sharing modern-day "Job" stories.

Will God Heal Me? by Ronald Dunn (Multnomah Books, 1997). A scriptural dissertation on healing, including a chapter on the doctrine of atonement healing. It's especially helpful for those who've been told that healing is guaranteed if they only believe.

1 You can learn more about the National Coalition for Cancer Survivorship at http://www.cansearch.org.

2 The National Cancer Institute Office of Cancer Survivorship can be accessed at http://dccps.nci.nih.gov/ocs/definitions.html.

3 *Webster's Seventh Collegiate*, s.v. "paranoid."

4 Actually 64% of adult cancer patients are still alive five years after diagnosis, according to a June 2004 report released by the National Cancer Institute and the Centers for Disease Control and Prevention. Statistics for childhood cancers are even more encouraging.

5 William Backus and Marie Chapian, *Telling Yourself the Truth* (Minneapolis: Bethany House Publishers, 2000), 21, italics in original.

6 M. Scott Peck, *Further Along the Road Less Traveled* (New York: Touchstone, 1993), 23.

7 Florence Ditlow, "The Missing Element in Health Care: Humor as a Form of Creativity," *Journal of Holistic Nursing* 11, no. 1, 66–79 (1993). See abstract at http://jhn.sagepub.com/cgi/content/abstract/11/1/66.

8 *The Encourager* newsletter, vol. 5, no. 4, Fall 1999, "Laughter Calisthenics," 5.

9 Rick Warren, *The Purpose-Driven Life* (Grand Rapids, MI: Zondervan, 2002), 202.

10 Max Lucado, *When God Whispers Your Name* (Dallas: Word Publishing, 1994), 73–74.

11 Jimmie Holland and Sheldon Lewis, *The Human Side of Cancer: Living with Hope, Coping with Uncertainty* (New York: HarperCollins, 2001), 14.

12 Ibid., 30–31.

13 Ibid.

14 Joni Eareckson Tada, "A List of Tears" in *More Precious Than Silver* (Grand Rapids: Zondervan, 1998), April 24. Thanks to Joni for encouraging me and other readers of this devotional to consider the many reasons we've shed tears over the years.

15 Rick Warren, *The Purpose-Driven Life*, 202.

16 Larry Keefauver, *When God Doesn't Heal Now* (Nashville: Thomas Nelson, 2000), 103.

17 Read more about why feathers and Psalm 91:4 meant so much to Carollynn at http://www.featherfund.org/the_story.htm.

Cancer survivors have unique needs.

Those facing cancer right now

need God's presence in a different way.

When God & Cancer Meet
by Lynn Eib

Softcover—$12.99
ISBN-13: 978-0-8423-7015-8
ISBN-10: 0-8423-7015-3

From acclaimed author Lynn Eib,
a powerful resource for anyone currently facing cancer